SEEDS
OF
STILLNESS

This book is a work of reflective nonfiction and creative spiritual writing. While it
draws on universal themes, psychological insight, and symbolic traditions, it is not
intended as a substitute for professional mental health, medical, or legal advice.

First Edition
ISBN: 978-1-7638934-6-7
Cover design and interior layout by Aussie Guys Books
Edited and published by Aussie Guys Books

For permissions, speaking engagements, and upcoming releases, visit:
www.aussieguysbooks.com.au

365 Days of SOUL™ is a trademark of Jason A. Solomon.

365 DAYS OF SOUL
VOLUME 1

JANUARY

FEBRUARY

MARCH

Your Journey Through Time, Shadow, and Spirit

Explore each day as a mirror of meaning, growth, and healing.

Jason A. Solomon

Titles in Series
365 Days of SOUL

Welcome to Volume 1

SEEDS
OF
STILLNESS

*Your spiritual companion for
the first breath of every day*

*Before the world reaches you... reach for yourself.
This book is your sacred space to begin again:
~ gently, quietly, and with soul ~*

How to Use Your Book

Seeds of Stillness is the first volume in the *365 Days of SOUL* series ~ a tender collection of daily reflections, poetic parables, and grounding insights that invite you to meet the day with clarity, care, and conscious presence.

— It is NOT a calendar, it is a rhythm

— It is spiritual support

— An emotional anchor and

— Inner wisdom

All designed to awaken your soul before your schedule.

Each entry is crafted for the first moment of your day ~ before you check your phone, before the headlines, even before you get out of bed.

For each day, you'll find:

— A Soul Story or Symbolic Parable ~ to reflect your emotional season

— The Daily Archetype ~ a part of you emerging today

— Sacred Wisdom ~ drawn from nature, spiritual traditions, and Eastern philosophy

— A Reflection Prompt to deepen your awareness

— A Sacred Action a gentle practice for the day ahead

— A Mantra or Visual Cue to root the day's message

Read. Breathe. Reflect. Begin Again.

Even a single paragraph can shift your day, not through pressure, but through *presence*.

Seasonal Awareness

Whether you're in the Northern Hemisphere blooming into spring, or the Southern Hemisphere softening into autumn, this book honours both cycles.

Each entry reflects your *inner season* as well ~ moments of growth, letting go, courage, stillness, and spiritual remembrance.

Why Begin with Stillness?

Because stillness is not emptiness. ~ It is *arrival*. Stillness is how you remember the truth before the world asks you to forget.

— Let this be the first voice you hear.

— Let these pages become your soft foundation.

— Let your soul greet the day before the world greets you.

———————————— ⌘ ————————————

*"You do not need to strive to awaken,
you only need to remember to begin,
in stillness."*

Contents

Welcome to your morning sanctuary.

Welcome to yourself.

January 1 - The Day of Sacred Beginning

A Soul Parable of Stillness, Listening, and the Truth Beneath the Surface

There once was a soul who had travelled far ~ too far, perhaps ~ in search of something it couldn't name. Each year, it arrived at the same place: a new day wrapped in quiet expectation, its spirit heavy with intentions and goals. *"This time,"* it whispered, *"I will get it right."*

But this year, something changed.

As the sun rose on the first day of the year, the soul did not make a list. It didn't rush into movement. It did not strive. Instead, it stepped outside, into the pale breath of winter, and simply stood ~ not to begin, but to listen.

There, in the hush between one year and the next, it heard something low and ancient stirring beneath the frost-covered earth. It pressed its ear gently to the soil. And in the silence, it heard the whisper of roots stretching deep and slow beneath the surface:

"You are already becoming."

That was all. Not a shout. Not a plan. Just a truth, soft and sacred.

The soul wept ~ not from sadness, but from relief. The pressure of beginning had lifted. The striving had lost its shape. What remained was presence.

In the world of symbols, today is marked by the number 1 ~ a number of fresh starts, yes, but also of individual essence.

It is the spark before the flame, the breath before the movement. Beneath today's Capricorn sun, the message is not ambition, but alignment. What matters now is not how far you run, but how deeply you root.

In the east, farmers once waited through still winters with patience. They did not demand fruit from frozen trees. They trusted that beneath the quiet, life was arranging itself.

And so the soul walked through a bare field ~ no blooms, no bursting life, only wind and breath and soft ground. Yet something moved beneath it all. The soul felt this. And as it reached a still clearing, it realized:

"We do not begin in brightness. We begin in stillness."

It closed its eyes and saw itself clearly ~ not as a warrior charging into a new year, but as a seed, small and full of silent purpose, wrapped in the spiral of potential.

This seed had an archetype ~ a name whispered from deep time: The Seed Bearer. This one knows how to carry what is not yet visible, what is sacred and unspoken, but entirely alive.

The symbols surrounding the soul shifted. A tortoise emerged from the underbrush, moving with unwavering patience.

A crystal of smoky quartz shimmered with grounding light. And far off, a tarot card floated into vision ~ The Fool, pure and open, walking without certainty but full of trust.

The soul understood: today was not a test. It was a threshold.

In the heart of this threshold lies a healing ~ especially for those who were once made to believe they must earn their worth by doing. The soul remembered old stories: times it had been driven to perform, to be perfect, to produce. But those stories faded now.

This day was not a page to fill. It was a space to breathe.

It placed a hand over its chest and asked, *"What part of me needs to be held as I begin?"*

The answer was small. Simple. Honest. And enough. "I do not rush the sacred. I begin by being." The soul wrote this softly into the earth and exhaled.

Later, as twilight returned, the soul lit a single candle ~ not as a resolution, but as a reverent flame. It whispered to no one and everyone at once:

"I am here. I begin." Then it sat with a pen in hand and listened again ~ not for answers, but for reflection.

— What would it mean to begin without urgency?

— What part of me is asking to start slowly ~ to be witnessed, not rushed?

— What would it feel like to trust the quiet?

In response, it drew a spiral. A pause. A seed. This was its beginning. Not a bang. Not a roar. But a sacred root curling into place. Deep. Quiet. Real.

"You don't have to leap today," the soul remembered.

"You only have to arrive."

Today, let yourself write not with urgency, but with intimacy.

Let this be your sacred pause ~ a place to *witness yourself*, rather than plan who you think you must become.

Journal Prompts:

— Where in my life am I being called to begin again ~ not with effort, but with presence?

— What if I trusted that I'm already in motion, even if I cannot see it?

— What does it feel like to begin slowly ~ to let my becoming take root beneath the surface?

If words don't come, draw a spiral. A seed. A small candle. Let that be enough. This is not about expression. It's about *remembering.*

Sacred Actions:

Before anything else today ~ before screens, schedules, or speech ~ light a single candle.

Sit beside it in stillness for 3 minutes. As it burns, whisper:

"I do not rush the sacred. I begin by being."

Let this become your morning ritual for as long as you need. This flame is not a goal. It is a witness to your presence.

Your Mantra for Today ~

"I do not leap into the year.

I arrive in it ~ slowly, wholly, sacredly."

January 2 - The Day of Gentle Presence

A quiet unfolding into tenderness, attunement, and embodied awareness

There once was a soul who had spent much of their life reaching for something beyond the moment. Always planning. Always adjusting. Always asking, *"What next?"* It was not a fault ~ only a habit born of fear. The fear that rest might be mistaken for laziness. That stillness might be mistaken for absence. That softness might go unseen.

But today was different.

Today, the soul awoke and did not rush. It didn't check the time. It didn't check the lists. It simply sat with the sunlight pouring gently through the curtains and whispered to the morning:

"Let me meet this day without forcing it."

There was something sacred in that softness ~ a feeling of being exactly where one needed to be.

Numerologically, the energy of 2 brings attunement (harmony), sensitivity, and relational presence. It asks us not to charge forward, but to *coexist*. It's the number of partnerships, of inner balance, and of learning to respond rather than react. Today is a mirror, reflecting the quiet beauty in how you *are*, not what you *do*.

In the zodiac, the Capricorn sun continues to hold us in earthy steadiness, but January 2 brings in a more feminine, yin-like current ~ inviting reflection, embodiment, and connection with subtlety over structure.

The soul rose slowly, walked barefoot across the floor, and stepped outside where the ground was still cool with dew. It stood there ~ no shoes, no shield ~ just skin on earth.

It listened.

Birdsong far off. The breath of trees. A cloud shifting. Nothing dramatic. And yet everything mattered.

This was presence ~ not practiced, not polished. Just... real.

"You don't need to rise loudly," the earth seemed to say. "Rising softly is still rising."

The soul thought of its past, and how often it had only felt seen when it was giving ~ offering, helping, producing. But what if today was about receiving? Receiving the moment, the light, the air, the enoughness of simply *being here*?

The archetype of this day is The Gentle Witness ~ one who sees without grasping, holds without squeezing, and loves without proving. A presence that nourishes just by showing up fully.

The symbols around this soul took shape like memory returning:

— A deer, quiet and alert, graceful in its watchfulness

— A rose quartz crystal, humming with unconditional self-acceptance

— A single card: The High Priestess, keeper of silence, intuition, and mystery

In the world of healing, today touches the wounds of invisibility ~ of not being met in your quiet. If you were only affirmed when loud, when useful, or when "on," then today is medicine. Today says:

"You are enough, exactly as you are. Even in your quiet."

The soul breathed this in deeply. It placed its hand over its heart and asked, not with urgency, but with care:

"What is it like to simply let myself be loved ~ here, now, softly?"

No answer came. Only a feeling ~ like silk settling over skin.

That was enough.

Later, the soul sat down with pen and page and let the day speak through reflection:

— Where do I still equate gentleness with weakness?

— What happens when I don't try to lead the moment, but just be in it?

— How does the world feel when I stop bracing against it?

As the sun drifted lower in the sky, the soul lit no candle this time. It opened a window. Let in the air. The breeze touched its face like an old friend.

There was no need to declare. Just to dwell. Just to be.

"Gentleness," it realized, "is the strength I was never taught to trust."

And in that knowing, the day became complete.

Your Mantra for Today ~

"My presence is enough. I offer it gently."

January 3 - The Day of Silent Intention

A story of inner clarity, wordless will, and the power of invisible alignment

There once was a soul who used to believe that declarations made things real. That if it didn't say it aloud, post it, write it on a board or speak it into a crowd ~ it wouldn't count.

But there came a time ~ maybe today ~ when the soul discovered something else entirely.

It woke early, before the rest of the world stirred. The sky outside was still a deep blue-grey, as if the sun had not yet remembered its purpose. There was no noise. Just the pulse of the breath. The weight of the blanket. The quiet presence of being.

And somewhere in that stillness, a decision was made.

Not a loud one. Not a resolution. Not even a word. Just a turning. A shift in the soil beneath the soul's inner roots. A *yes* so quiet it didn't even echo.

"Not all intentions need to be spoken," the soul realized. "Some are meant to be *lived into*."

Today holds the energy of the number 3 ~ a number of creativity, communication, and growth. But in this season of stillness, its invitation is more inward. Less about output, more about clarity. The kind of clarity that doesn't require proof. Just presence.

The soul made tea, slowly. There was a sacredness in each motion ~ in the pour, in the steeping, in the steam rising in silence.

No big ideas. No dramatic commitments. Just a quiet *knowing* blooming at the center of the chest.

This is what it meant to carry silent intention ~ to be in alignment with something deeper than goal-setting.

Under the Capricorn sun, January 3 whispers about discipline without noise, direction without announcement, and devotion without performance.

It is a day to practice still resolve.

The archetype walking beside this soul is The Inner Flame Keeper ~ one who tends the fire no one sees, the one who stokes a vision slowly and patiently, without fanfare or applause.

The symbols around this day are powerful in their simplicity:

— A lantern, glowing dimly but steady in the dark

— A flint stone, silent and sharp, used only when ready

— A card from the deck: The Hermit ~ guide of the quiet path

— A crystal: Labradorite, protector of inner truth and mystery

The healing embedded in this day is for those who were once told: *"If you don't say it, it doesn't matter."* Or, *"If you don't declare it, you won't commit."*

But some commitments grow best in the dark. Like seeds.

And today, the soul learns that not all clarity requires a conversation. Some intentions are soul-deep ~ private, protected, powerful.

"Let your intention be a lantern," the soul thought. "Even if no one sees you carrying it."

Later that day, the soul sat with its journal ~ not to write a plan, but to listen.

— What am I quietly committing to?

— Where in my life do I feel the shift before I see it?

— How can I honor what I know without needing others to validate it?

There was peace in these questions. Not answers ~ but space. As twilight arrived, the soul lit a small flame. Not for show. Just for the self.

It did not say a word. It simply breathed and knew: *I am in motion, even in silence.*

Symbolic Focus: The breath held between inhale and exhale. The pause before speech.

Your Mantra for Today ~

"My intention does not need to be loud to be real."

January 4 - The Day of Rooted Resolve

A parable of quiet determination, anchored identity, and strength beneath the surface

There was once a soul that had confused resolve with resistance.

It believed that to be strong, one must be hard. That to be committed, one must be loud. That to hold to a path, one must clench their jaw and press forward.

But then came a day ~ cool and clear ~ where the earth whispered a different truth.

The soul had wandered into a forest in the early morning, unsure why. The trees stood like ancient monks ~ tall, unmoving, unafraid. There was no urgency among them, no sprinting toward the light. Only steadiness. Presence. Patience.

The soul leaned against the bark of an old tree and listened ~ not with its ears, but with its bones. And deep within the silence, it heard:

"You do not need to force what is already rooted."

The number 4, holding today's energy, is the number of foundation, structure, and inner pillars. But it is not rigid ~ it is dependable. Not controlling ~ but centered. Today asks us to explore the difference between *pushing forward* and *standing firm*.

The Capricorn sun holds this day in sacred gravity. There is no rushing here. No drama. Just the slow, deliberate formation of stability.

The soul sat at the base of the tree. It remembered all the times it had tried to prove its worth by effort ~ by overwork, by anxiety masked as discipline. But now, something shifted. It felt its own spine aligned with the tree trunk. Something clicked. A truth emerged:

"Rootedness is not stillness. It is readiness."

The soul breathed deeper, exhaled slower, and felt its resolve soften into something stronger ~ not brittle willpower, but living commitment.

Today, the archetype that walks beside you is The Steady One ~ the soul who returns to their truth again and again, not with a roar, but with a step. And then another. And another.

Your symbols today speak to depth, anchoring, and faith in the invisible:

— Tree roots, spiralling and stretching deep into unseen soil

— Obsidian, the dark crystal of protection and grounding

— The Four of Wands, a tarot card of stable joy and soul-built foundation

— And the elephant, wise, immovable, quietly mighty

This day carries a gentle but powerful healing for those who feel they've had to perform strength. If you were taught that resolve meant tension, today offers a new way: strength without struggle.

"Let your power be steady," the soul reminded itself. "Let your truth be a place you return to, not a thing you chase."

In the stillness of the afternoon, the soul lit a candle and placed a small stone beside it. No declarations. No demands. Just an offering of commitment ~ to the path it already chose long ago.

— Where in my life am I confusing tension for strength?

— What roots am I ready to grow deeper, not wider?

— What does steady devotion feel like in my body?

There were no revelations. Just the feeling of anchoring. The soul did not need to say it was ready. It already was.

Symbolic Focus: The spine, the feet, the pause between commitment and action.

Your Mantra for Today ~

"I do not rush forward. I root down."

January 5 - The Day of Inner Listening

*A story of quiet signals,
hidden truths, and the courage
to hear what's already within*

There was a soul who had grown up believing that answers lived outside of them.

So they listened ~ not to themselves, but to the noise. To the opinions. The expectations. The subtle and not-so-subtle commands of the world: *"Be like this." "Do that." "Don't speak too loud." "Don't shrink too small."*

And so, over time, their own inner voice became a whisper too faint to follow.

But today, that whisper begins to rise.

The soul sat quietly by a window as the winter light moved across the floor. The world was not asking anything of them yet. It was early. Still. Sacred.

And from somewhere within ~ not the mind, but the marrow ~ came a soundless message. It was not a sentence. Not even a thought. It was more like a pulse. A pull. A knowing.

"Listen here," it said. "Inside. Not out."

January 5 holds the energy of the number 5 ~ the number of the senses, of exploration, and personal freedom. But today, its wild energy turns inward. Instead of external experience, it invites *inner sensing*. The clarity that comes when you stop chasing signs and start *hearing yourself*.

The Capricorn sun remains, offering the container for grounded listening. Not fantasy. Not guesswork. But *truth* ~ the kind that comes when the noise fades.

The soul touched their chest, then their throat. Noticing what stirred when they sat with silence. There was grief there. There was wisdom, too.

The voice within didn't shout. It didn't try to convince. It simply *was* ~ waiting to be heard.

The archetype of the day is The Deep Listener ~ one who holds still long enough to hear what others overlook, including their own soul.

The symbols surrounding this moment gathered gently:

—   A stethoscope, not for the body, but the heart's quietest truths

—   Blue lace agate, a crystal of soft expression and inner calm

—   The Page of Cups, young and open to messages from the deep

—   A whale, whose song echoes through vast oceans, ancient and sure

This day carries healing for those who were taught that others always knew better ~ that their own inner compass couldn't be trusted.

If your trauma came through suppression, gaslighting, or emotional dismissal, this day is a reclamation.

"You are not too much for your truth," the soul reminded itself.

"You are simply learning to listen again."

The soul found a quiet space and placed one hand over their ear and the other over their heart. They didn't need to meditate or force awareness. They simply breathed. And in the space between inhale and exhale, they asked:

"What is my inner voice trying to tell me ~ that I keep ignoring?"

There was no explosion. No flood. Just a single word that rose like steam from still water.

They wrote it down. Then listened again.

Journal Prompts:

— What is trying to get my attention ~ inside me ~ right now?

— Where do I still seek outside validation for something I feel?

— What truth of mine has been waiting patiently to be heard?

Sacred Actions: Turn off all external sound ~ and sit in silence for 5 minutes. Just listen. Not for anything. Just *to* everything.

Symbolic Focus: The ears, the throat, and the space behind the sternum.

Your Mantra for Today ~

"I do not need to speak first. I need to listen deeper."

January 6 - The Day of Unfolding Light

A parable of emerging truth, inner radiance, and the slow reveal of what's always been

There once was a soul who had been hiding their light ~ not because it wasn't bright, but because somewhere along the way, they were taught to dim it.

Maybe someone told them they were "too much."

Maybe they felt unsafe shining.

Maybe no one saw them when they did.

So the soul learned to fold its light inward, like a lantern wrapped in layers of cloth. Protected. Dimmed. Deferred.

But on this day ~ a morning quiet with frost and sky-silver air ~ something began to shift.

The soul stepped outside, bundled and uncertain, and watched as the pale sun emerged slowly through the mist. It didn't burst forth. It didn't announce itself. It simply revealed ~ moment by moment ~ the warmth it had been carrying all along.

"Ah," thought the soul, "That is how I want to return ~ not in a blaze, but in a blooming."

Today carries the energy of the number 6 ~ the number of healing, harmony, and returning to the self with compassion. It asks not for grand displays, but for softness. For integration. For allowing.

Under the Capricorn sun, this light is not superficial. It's earned through stillness, made visible through trust, and offered through grace.

The soul felt something stir inside ~ a kind of unfolding in the chest, like petals that had been clenched in defense beginning to part.

This wasn't about "shining bright" to be seen. It wasn't about performance. It was about *allowing what is already present to emerge* ~ slowly, naturally, in its own time.

The archetype that guides this day is The Inner Flame Tender ~ one who does not rush the fire but coaxes it gently back to life.

The symbols gathered with gentleness and intention:

- A lotus, rising from the mud, opening one petal at a time
- Sunstone, a crystal of vitality and warmth that doesn't demand, but invites
- The Six of Pentacles, reminding us that balance isn't just about giving, it's about receiving the right to radiate
- A moth, drawn toward light, not recklessly, but instinctively

This day brings healing for those who've suppressed joy, pride, or visibility for the sake of safety, humility, or silence. If your glow was once mocked, ignored, or punished, today whispers:

"It's safe now. You do not have to burst. You can simply unfold."

Later, the soul sat with a journal and a golden thread from a craft box they hadn't opened in years. They wrapped the thread around their wrist and wrote:

— What part of me is ready to emerge?

— What would it look like to let my joy be seen not all at once, but slowly?

— Where have I mistaken humility for hiding?

They didn't force answers. They just breathed. And little by little, something warm moved upward through their spine.

Sacred Actions: Stand near a source of natural light today. Let it touch your face. Whisper to yourself:

"I allow the light within me to unfold. Nothing rushed. Nothing hidden."

Symbolic Focus: The chest center, the fingertips, and the sensation of warmth meeting cool.

Your Mantra for Today ~

"My light returns in its own rhythm. I do not rush it. I welcome it."

January 7 - The Day of Grounded Vision

A story of rooted foresight, sacred planning, and clarity held without urgency

There once was a soul who had many visions.

Beautiful ones. Big ones. Wild ones. They would come in dreams, in sparks of inspiration, in sudden ideas scrawled across napkins and notebooks and margins of other plans.

But none of them ever seemed to land. They floated ~ inspiring, fleeting, untethered.

And so, over time, the soul grew weary. *"What good is vision,"* it wondered, *"if it never becomes something real?"*

On this day, the soul wandered into a valley surrounded by stone. The ground was solid beneath them. No shifting sands. No fog. Just earth ~ present, wide, supportive.

The wind whispered gently through the canyon walls:

"Your vision is not lost. It simply needs ground."

That's when the soul remembered: Dreams are seeds. Without soil, they never root.

Today is carried by the energy of the number 7 ~ the number of spiritual insight, deep reflection, and inner clarity. It invites us to see beyond the surface, but not to escape it. Instead, to anchor that vision into the body, the breath, the ground beneath our feet.

Under the Capricorn sun, the message becomes even clearer: Long-term vision is sacred ~ but only when it's built on something real.

The soul sat with this, feeling into its spine, its feet. It placed its hand on its belly ~ the center of trust ~ and asked:

"What vision lives in me that I am ready to hold with both grace and grit?"

It didn't need a ten-step plan. Not yet. Just clarity. Just anchoring. Just willingness.

The archetype of the day is The Architect of the Soul ~ one who sees what could be, but doesn't float away with the image. They draw it down, they shape it, they walk it into being.

Today's symbols arise like blueprints from the earth:

— A mountain, unmoving yet visionary

— Hematite, the crystal of grounding clarity and protected focus

— The Knight of Pentacles, steady in pace, committed in purpose

— A raven, bringing messages of long-range insight, grounded in wisdom

Today's healing is for the dreamers who have felt lost in their own imagination. For the ones who've seen clearly what could be ~ but were never taught how to hold it in their hands.

"You are not wrong for seeing far," the soul reminded itself. "You simply need to bring your feet with you."

As dusk neared, the soul lit a candle and placed a stone beside a sketch ~ not of a finished plan, but of a foundation.

It wrote slowly, intentionally:

— What vision in me is ready to take root?

— Where have I floated too high without anchoring down?

— What daily steps, small and sacred, would honor this dream?

The answers came in stillness, not certainty.

Sacred Actions: Take one small, grounded step today toward a long-held vision. Write it, name it, walk it, plan it ~ but do it with presence, not pressure.

Symbolic Focus: The feet, the lower back, the hands that shape what is imagined.

Your Mantra for Today ~

"My vision grows where I plant it. I anchor what I see."

January 8 - The Day of Quiet Power

A story of still presence, inner strength, and the force that doesn't shout

There once was a soul who believed power had to be loud.

They were told that power looked like command, sounded like certainty, moved like momentum. So they tried to become that ~ louder, faster, firmer. And for a time, it worked. People listened. People followed.

But inside, something felt hollow. Performance was mistaken for purpose. Volume had become a shield.

And then came this day ~ a day with no expectation, no platform, no need to prove.

The soul found itself standing beside a boulder. Nothing moved. The air was still. But the presence of that stone was undeniable.

No one questioned its strength. No one doubted its place.

It simply existed, fully ~ not forcing, not shrinking.

"This," the soul thought, "is power ~ not in dominance, but in essence."

Today carries the vibration of the number 8 ~ the number of power, authority, and aligned strength. But true 8-energy isn't about control ~ it's about integrity. Inner congruence. Wholeness that doesn't need to shout.

Under the watchful Capricorn sun, today is less about what you show and more about what you *embody*. It's the strength of silence. The power of restraint. The quiet certainty that says:

"I am here. That is enough."

The archetype of the day is The Pillar ~ the soul that does not waver with winds, nor seek to tower over others. They stand in their truth because it is theirs ~ not because they need it to be seen.

Today's symbols form a strong and still constellation:

— A stone altar, grounded and weathered

— Black tourmaline, a crystal of protection and energetic sovereignty

— The Strength card, not the brute, but the graceful lion-tamer within

— An elephant, whose presence is undeniable, and movements are deliberate

This day offers healing to those who equate power with pressure. If your strength has been misused, misunderstood, or mistaken for harshness, today says:

"You do not need to roar to be powerful. You do not need to carry others to be strong."

The soul took time to pause. Not to think. Not to meditate. Just to *be*.

Feet flat. Spine tall. No words. No action. Only embodiment.

It lit no candle. It made no vow.

It simply let its own grounded presence take up space ~ as naturally as a stone resting in the earth.

Then, when the time felt right, it picked up the journal and asked:

— Where in my life do I confuse power with performance?

— What does quiet strength feel like in my body today?

— Where can I lead without pushing?

Sacred Actions: Choose silence today in one place where you'd normally speak or explain. Not as avoidance ~ but as embodied knowing.

Symbolic Focus: The root chakra, the spine, and the hands resting on the thighs.

Your Mantra for Today ~

"My power is not in proving. My power is in presence."

January 9 - The Day of Soul Recall

A story of remembering what never left, and the deep wisdom buried beneath forgetting

There once was a soul who couldn't remember who they were.

Not on the surface ~ their name, their job, their daily roles were all intact. But somewhere deeper, they felt scattered. Disconnected. As though a part of them had drifted away over time ~ not lost, just distant.

They didn't know when it happened. Was it the moment they chose silence over truth? The year they buried their joy to survive? The season they stopped listening to the pull inside?

They couldn't say.

But on this day ~ quiet, overcast, unremarkable by the world's standards ~ something stirred. Not loudly. Not dramatically. Just… insistently.

A tug. A scent. A shiver in the chest. And the soul heard it:

"Come back."

It was not a reprimand. Not a guilt-trip. It was a call ~ loving, ancestral, unmistakable.

"Come back to who you were before the forgetting."

Today holds the vibration of the number 9 ~ the number of completion, spiritual return, and integration of the long journey. It is the wise elder in the cycle, not looking to begin again but to gather what has already been scattered and bring it home.

Under Capricorn's sturdy gaze, this energy isn't airy or mystical. It is grounded remembrance. Embodied soul memory. It invites you to retrieve what is yours ~ the truth of you, before the roles, the wounds, the adjustments.

The archetype of the day is The Soul Rememberer ~ one who carries the thread of their true self even through lifetimes of forgetting, and who knows that to return is not to rewind ~ it is to reclaim.

The symbols of this day gather gently, like a fog lifting from a familiar path:

— A mirror in still water, where your reflection stares back wiser than before

— Lapis lazuli, stone of memory and divine lineage

— The Judgement card in tarot, not of punishment, but of *awakening*

— A crane, who returns to the same place year after year, guided by knowing

This day carries healing for those who have abandoned themselves to belong, adapted themselves to survive, or dulled their voice to be accepted. It reminds us:

"Your soul never disappeared. It just dimmed for a while. But it remembers."

The soul knelt near a river that morning and looked at the reflection ~ not to critique, but to witness.

They whispered a name they hadn't used in years. Not their given name ~ but the one only their heart remembered.

Tears came. But not of pain. Of reunion.

Journal Prompts:

— What parts of me have I forgotten or silenced to fit in or

feel safe?

— What calls me back to myself right now?

— Who was I before the world told me who to be?

Sacred Actions: Take a few minutes to close your eyes and whisper to yourself, either aloud or in thought:

"I remember." Let it be enough. Let what rises be sacred.

Symbolic Focus: The third eye, the heart, the base of the skull.

Your Mantra for Today ~

"I return to what I never truly left. I remember my soul."

January 10 - The Day of Breath and Belonging

A story of coming home to the body, the breath, and the invisible thread that connects us all

There once was a soul who had spent most of their life holding their breath.

Not consciously. Not in protest. Just… out of habit. The kind of holding that comes from bracing ~ for judgment, for disappointment, for the next demand.

The kind of holding that makes your chest tighten and your voice tremble.

The kind that says, *"It's not safe to fully be here."*

But on this day, something changed.

The soul awoke before dawn, wrapped in a quiet that felt different ~ not hollow, but holy. They stepped outside and met the morning air with an inhale that didn't flinch.

The breath was deeper than usual. Slower. Like it came from somewhere older than lungs.

And with that breath came a sensation they hadn't felt in years:

Belonging.

Not to a place. Not to a title. Not to someone else's expectations.

But to life itself.

"I belong because I exist," the soul thought. "Not because I earn it."

Today carries the number 10, which holds the fullness of a cycle. It's the 1 of a new beginning, amplified by the 0 of infinite potential. Together, they invite you to start fresh ~ not from pressure, but from wholeness.

Under the Capricorn sun, January 10 grounds that truth into the body. It reminds you that the first home is *not a house.* It is the breath. It is the skin. It is the beating heart that never stopped calling you back.

The archetype of the day is The Embodied One ~ the soul who returns to the wisdom of their breath as a sacred compass, and who belongs not because they are perfect, but because they are present.

Today's symbols come wrapped in warmth and return:

— A circle of stones, steady and unbroken

— Rose quartz, the crystal of unconditional self-acceptance

— The Ten of Cups, symbol of inner and outer harmony

— A wolf, belonging to its pack and also to the wilderness itself

This day offers healing for those who've felt like they never fit. For the ones who were told they were "too much" or "not enough." For the ones who thought they had to shrink or shapeshift just to be allowed a place.

"You belong here," the day whispers. "You have always belonged."

The soul placed a hand on their chest and another on their belly. They inhaled. Then again. Slower. Deeper.

And something clicked ~ not in the mind, but in the body.

They didn't need to explain their presence. They were already home.

Journal Prompts:

— Where do I still hold my breath out of fear or habit?

— What would it feel like to be fully here, in this moment, in this body?

— How can I remind myself that belonging begins with me?

Sacred Actions: Pause three times today and take five slow breaths. With each exhale, whisper to yourself: "I belong." Let your body hear it. Let your nervous system believe it.

Symbolic Focus: The lungs, the diaphragm, the skin between collarbones.

Mantra for the Day:

"With each breath, I return to myself. I belong here."

January 11 - The Day of Inner Alignment

A story of centering, coherence, and the quiet strength of living in your own rhythm

There once was a soul who had lived in fragments.

They were kind in one room, sharp in another. Confident in their work, but uncertain at home. Wise in solitude, but lost in a crowd. They wore many faces ~ not out of dishonesty, but survival.

They had become skilled at reading the room, adapting to fit, bending without breaking.

But something was missing.

A thread. A throughline. A place where all parts of them could meet and say, *"Yes. This is me."*

Then came this day ~ cold and clear ~ where the soul stopped moving. Not out of exhaustion, but out of clarity.

They stood in front of a mirror and didn't just look ~ they *listened*.

And from somewhere deep within came a quiet alignment, like bones settling into place.

"Let all of me face the same direction," the soul whispered. "Let my thoughts, my actions, and my truth come into one line."

Today is guided by the master number 11 ~ a number of intuition, illumination, and alignment between the earthly and the spiritual. It's a bridge number ~ connecting realms, selves, intentions.

Under the Capricorn sun, it becomes practical mysticism ~ alignment not just as a feeling, but as a path.

Today, the soul is asked not to strive, but to *integrate*. To become congruent. To bring the inner compass to the surface and follow it, faithfully.

The archetype that rises here is The Soul Aligner ~ one who lives with integrity so complete, their presence calms the room without effort.

The symbols of this day hold symmetry and quiet power:

— A vertical beam of light, extending from crown to ground

— Clear quartz, magnifier of truth and amplifier of purpose

— The Justice card, representing clarity, choice, and energetic balance

— A crane, standing on one leg with infinite poise, perfectly still

Today offers healing for those who've contorted themselves to fit others' needs. For those who've hidden pieces of themselves just to feel safe. For those who have been misaligned, not by fault, but by necessity.

"You do not need to split yourself to be loved," the day whispers.
"You are not too many pieces. You are one sacred whole."

The soul sat cross-legged on the floor, spine upright, hands resting on knees ~ not in performative meditation, but in honest alignment.

They didn't need mantras or affirmations. Just breath. Just body. Just *truth*.

Then came the questions:

— Where in my life am I not aligned with my inner truth?

— What would it mean to move, speak, and choose from the same center?

— What part of me is ready to stop bending?

No answers were rushed. But the body softened. The mind cleared. The spirit settled into place.

Sacred Actions: Stand with your feet hip-width apart. Close your eyes. Imagine a thread from crown to root. Inhale up, exhale down. Whisper:

"I bring all parts of me into alignment."

Symbolic Focus: The spine, the third eye, the center of the chest.

Your Mantra for Today ~

"I align. I listen. I live from center."

January 12 - The Day of Threshold Energy

A story of transition, sacred in-between moments, and the courage to step without certainty

There once was a soul who had lived most of their life on the edge of things.

Too old for one chapter, not quite ready for the next. Too healed to go back, still too tender to move forward. They lived in the hallway ~ in that liminal space where nothing was fixed, and everything felt unknown.

And so they waited. And waited. Hoping that clarity would arrive like a letter under the door.

But on this day ~ cool and filled with a soft hum in the air ~ the soul realized something quietly life-changing:

"The threshold is not a pause. It is a place."

It was not a mistake. Not a void. It was sacred architecture ~ the moment where oneself dissolves so another can emerge.

Today carries the vibration of the number 12, a sacred number found in the zodiac, the months of the year, the hours on a clock. It speaks of completion through transition, readiness through release, and the willingness to step even when you don't know what's on the other side.

Under Capricorn's guiding sun, today brings structure to uncertainty. It says: *"You don't need a map to begin. You only need a doorway and the will to walk through."*

The archetype of the day is The Threshold Keeper ~ one who honors the pause before the leap, who knows the space between no longer and not yet is holy.

The symbols of this day are ancient and powerful:

— A key, resting in an open palm

— Moonstone, for intuition, transition, and emotional flow

— The Two of Wands, the card of planning before action, doorway before departure

— A butterfly in chrysalis, not quite caterpillar, not yet winged

This day offers healing to those who have rushed through transitions out of fear or remained stuck in limbo out of doubt. If your trauma taught you that movement must be fast or not at all, today teaches a new rhythm.

"The threshold," the soul said, "is not where I lose myself. It is where I meet who I am becoming."

Later, the soul walked to a doorway in their own home. They didn't walk through it. They simply stood. One hand on the frame. One foot in. One foot out.

And they let the body feel it ~ that tension, that wonder, that stretch.

They let the moment *be*.

They asked themselves:

— What threshold am I standing on right now?
— What am I afraid to leave behind, even though I've already outgrown it?
— What does stepping forward ~ even slightly ~ feel like in my body?

And slowly, gently, they shifted their weight forward.

Sacred Actions: Choose a literal threshold in your home ~ a doorway, a gate, a crossing. Stand in it with intention. Breathe. Say aloud:

"I honor this space. I honor my crossing."

Symbolic Focus: The feet, the sacral center, the space just before movement.

Your Mantra for Today ~

"I am not lost. I am between."

January 13 - The Day of Invisible Strength

A story of quiet resilience, unseen endurance, and the power that lives beneath the surface

There once was a soul who had endured more than most could see.

They carried grief in their bones, silence in their throat, and storms in their chest ~ yet from the outside, they looked calm. Maybe even ordinary.

People admired their composure. Commented on their grace. But no one saw the weight they lifted simply by waking each day. No one noticed the victories hidden in the quiet.

Until today.

On this day, soft and grey, the soul walked by a frozen lake. The surface was still ~ unmoving. But they knew: just beneath that fragile layer, the water was alive. Flowing. Deep. Holding centuries of memory.

"So am I," the soul thought. "Still on the surface, but alive with strength no one sees."

The number 13, often misunderstood, is a number of transformation and inner power. It asks you to embrace what is hidden ~ the kind of strength forged not in noise, but in surviving, healing, and continuing.

Under the Capricorn sun, this energy finds form: it grounds the invisible into embodiment. It says, *"You don't need to prove your power. You already live it."*

The archetype of the day is The Silent Warrior ~ one who doesn't wear armor but carries endurance like breath. Who stands not to be seen, but because they know they cannot be broken.

The symbols of this day speak in whispers, not roars:

— A stone beneath water, unmoved by the current

— Obsidian, dark and protective, a guardian of deep truth

— The Strength card reversed ~ strength through surrender, not control

— A snow leopard, solitary and majestic, surviving in silence

This day brings healing for those who have been told: *"You're so strong,"* but never asked, *"Are you okay?"*

For those who've carried pain like a private contract. For those whose strength was built in silence.

"You don't owe anyone your strength," the day says. "But you deserve to honor it."

That evening, the soul lit a candle and placed beside it something symbolic ~ an old photograph, a worn journal, a stone from a time of difficulty.

They didn't tell the story aloud. They didn't explain. They simply *witnessed* themselves.

And Being honest with yourself, ask:

— Where have I been stronger than anyone knew?

— What do I need to say to the part of me that held it all together?

— How can I honor the strength that never asked to be tested, but survived anyway?

The answers came not in words, but in warmth. A softening in the chest. A loosening in the jaw.

The strength didn't need to fight anymore. It just needed to be seen.

Sacred Actions: Write a letter to your past self ~ the one who held it all together when no one noticed. Say thank you. Say sorry. Say whatever is true.

Symbolic Focus: The solar plexus, the lower back, the inner flame.

Your Mantra for Today ~

"I carry a strength the world may never see ~ but I see it now."

January 14 - The Day of Still Motion

A story of paradox, presence, and the rhythm that moves even when nothing changes

There once was a soul who believed growth meant movement ~ visible movement.

They measured their healing by how far they'd come. Their success by how much had changed. Their worth by how much they could show. And when life became still ~ unmoving, quiet, ordinary ~ they feared they were stuck.

But today was different.

The soul stood beside a quiet stream that barely moved. On the surface, it was still. But below? A soft current flowed ~ gentle, persistent, sure.

Something about it felt familiar.

They watched a single leaf float in place, held by invisible motion.

"What if stillness doesn't mean I've stopped?" the soul wondered.
"What if I'm being moved in ways I can't yet see?"

That thought caught something deep. They stayed longer, leaning into that still water with a quiet question rising.

What if the most important shifts… are the ones happening silently within?

The number 14 reduces to 5 ~ the number of changes, movement, and dynamic energy. But unlike chaotic change, this day speaks of subtle transformation. The kind you don't notice until suddenly, everything feels different.

Capricorn still governs the skies, offering patience and a foundation that honors slow unfolding.

The archetype of this day is The Watcher of Tides ~ the soul who learns to trust the current, even when it seems the tide isn't rising. They become fluent in the sacred language of *almosts*, *not yets*, and *soon*.

The symbols of the day hum with quiet momentum:

— A pendulum, swinging in soft rhythm

— Chrysoprase, a stone for gentle growth and heart-centered movement

— The Temperance card, alchemy through balance, transformation through presence

— A jellyfish, drifting yet carried ~ moving by trusting the sea itself

This day offers healing for those who equate stillness with stagnation. For those who panic when nothing seems to be happening. For those who once had to keep moving just to stay safe.

"Motion isn't always visible," the day says. "Some growth moves through your bones before it reaches your skin."

The soul returned home and didn't try to rush into something "productive." Instead, they sat, breathing. Sensing.

And in the middle of that quiet, a curiosity took hold:

If nothing were to change on the outside today… what inside me might begin to shift?

Journal Prompts:

— What stillness in my life do I mistake for failure?

— Where am I growing in ways I cannot yet see?

— What happens when I stop forcing forward motion?

Sacred Actions: Choose one task today to do slowly. Intentionally. Feel the rhythm of it. Let it be your meditation.

Symbolic Focus: The heart center, the breath, the space behind the navel.

Your Mantra for Today ~

"Even in stillness, I move."

January 15 - The Day of Earth Connection

A story of grounding, remembering your place, and the healing that comes when you touch the living world

There once was a soul who had forgotten the feel of soil.

They spent their days in climate control, surrounded by artificial light, walking on concrete and speaking through screens. Their life was fast, polished, efficient ~ but something inside felt... unrooted.

They didn't know they were missing the Earth ~ until they touched it again.

It happened on a morning they didn't expect. A walk, unplanned. A park bench, empty. A patch of grass, uneven and a little damp. And for some reason, they took off their shoes.

The cold met their skin. Not unpleasant ~ just real.

"This," the soul realized, "is what it feels like to be *here.*"

A wave rose in them ~ not of emotion, but of memory. A remembering older than their name. Older than this life.

A memory of belonging to the land. Of being held by it.

That single barefoot moment became a homecoming.

And yet ~ a question lingered:

What else have I forgotten that could root me, if I let it?

The number 15 reduces to 6, the number of harmony, healing, and returning to the heart. But today that return is physical ~ cellular. It is a somatic homecoming.

The Capricorn sun reinforces this, grounding the celestial in the material. The message is clear: *The body is not an inconvenience. It is the ritual.*

The archetype of the day is The Rooted Walker ~ one who remembers their soul through sensation, who carries their truth not just in thought, but in muscle, blood, and barefoot steps.

Symbols of the day bloom from the Earth itself:

— A circle of stones, ancient and unmoving

— Moss agate, a crystal of slow healing, growth, and Earth bonding

— The Queen of Pentacles, nurturing from grounded presence

— A bear, resting in winter, held by the rhythm of the land

Today offers healing for those who dissociated from the body to survive ~ who learned that stillness felt unsafe, or that presence was too overwhelming.

This day doesn't ask for perfection. Just *connection.*

"Come back into your skin," the day whispers. "There is medicine in your feet. There is knowing in your breath."

Later, the soul stood in their backyard and placed both hands on a tree trunk. Not to get anything. Not to say anything. Just to touch ~ and feel touched in return.

A breeze moved through their ribs. The roots beneath them seemed to pulse. Then came the thought:

If I really let myself be part of this Earth… what would shift in how I carry myself?

Journal Prompts:

— When do I feel most connected to the Earth ~ and how often do I let myself go there?

— What part of my body feels least "inhabited"? What happens when I breathe into it?

— What grounding practice is my body asking me to remember?

_____

_____

_____

_____

_____

_____

Sacred Actions: Take a walk barefoot, or sit with your spine against a tree. No phone. No agenda. Just contact. Let the Earth hold your attention.

Symbolic Focus: The soles of the feet, the tailbone, the back of the thighs.

Your Mantra for Today ~

"The Earth remembers me. I remember myself through her."

January 16 - The Day of Gentle Self-Compassion

A story of softness, healing through kindness, and the quiet revolution of treating yourself like someone you love

There once was a soul who was kind to everyone ~ except themselves.

They offered grace to others with ease. They forgave, soothed, and supported. But when it came to their own pain, their own mistakes, their own exhaustion? The voice shifted. It hardened. Turned sharp.

They didn't even realize it at first. That the way they spoke to themselves in private ~ they would *never* speak to someone they loved.

One morning, worn thin by invisible weight, the soul stood in front of the mirror with tired eyes and an even more tired heart. They expected the usual critique.

But instead ~ something unexpected happened.

They paused. Something inside said:

"Please… not today. Just be gentle with me."

That quiet plea cracked something open. And for the first time, the soul reached toward themselves with tenderness ~ not because they earned it, not because they did better, but simply because they *needed it*.

They placed a hand on their own cheek and whispered:

"I'm sorry I've been so hard on you. You didn't deserve that."

The number 16 reduces to 7, a number of spiritual insight and reflection. Today, it brings those qualities inward ~ to the hidden terrain of self-treatment. The message is simple but seismic:

You are not your inner critic. You are the one who gets to change the tone.

Under the Capricorn sun, today's energy becomes embodied: self-compassion not as a concept, but as a *practice*. As action. As sacred discipline.

The archetype of the day is The Inner Mother ~ the one who speaks to the wounded child within not with shame, but with warmth. The one who builds resilience through *gentle repair*.

The symbols of this day arrive softly:

— A wool blanket, warm and woven with care

— Pink opal, the crystal of emotional healing and heart support

— The Four of Swords, rest and self-recovery through loving boundaries

— A doe, cautious but brave, finding refuge in its own presence

And just as the soul felt their body begin to soften, a question surfaced that stopped them gently:

If I treated myself like someone I deeply loved… what would change today?

Later, the soul wrapped themselves in a scarf and brewed a cup of tea ~ not because they "deserved a treat," but because they *deserved care.*

They wrote slowly:

— Where have I been too harsh with myself lately?

— What am I afraid will happen if I soften?

— What kind of inner voice am I ready to begin listening to?

No performance. No judgment. Just noticing. Just being with themselves… kindly.

Sacred Actions: Place your hand over your heart. Say aloud, *"I offer myself kindness now ~ not as a reward, but as a way of being."* Then do one small thing for yourself that's purely for comfort.

Symbolic Focus: The chest center, the palms, the inner voice.

Your Mantra for Today ~

"I treat myself like someone I love."

January 17 - The Day of Root Medicine

A story of ancestral strength, foundational healing, and the wisdom found when you go deep instead of far

There once was a soul who kept looking up ~ toward goals, dreams, aspirations.

They reached for higher truths. Sought light. Sought expansion. They thought healing meant rising. That growth always moved upward.

But one day, the soul stumbled ~ not in defeat, but in surrender.

They fell to their knees in a quiet garden, hands pressing into the soil. And something unexpected happened: instead of shame or failure, they felt… anchored.

It wasn't the sky that spoke to them in that moment. It was the ground.

And what it said was this:

"Not all medicine rises. Some of it *roots*."

That single moment became a turning point. The soul began to wonder…

What if the strength I'm looking for isn't above me ~ but beneath me?

Today carries the number 17, which reduces to 8 ~ the number of power, structure, and embodied wisdom. But the power of this day is not about control. It's about anchoring into what *sustains you* ~ emotionally, spiritually, generationally.

Under the Capricorn sun, the invitation is unmistakable: Go deeper, not higher. Ground, then rise.

The archetype of the day is The Root Healer ~ one who nourishes from the base, tending to what was buried, forgotten, or passed down. They don't fear darkness. They know it is where true transformation begins.

Today's symbols bloom quietly underground:

— A root system, vast and unseen, holding the tree aloft

— Garnet, a crystal of grounding, blood memory, and vital force

— The Ace of Pentacles, a seed ready to take hold in sacred soil

— A mole, living beneath the surface, sensing through earth and instinct

This day offers healing for those whose foundations were shaky ~ who grew up fast, detached from roots, who survived by staying light, mobile, and untethered.

"To heal," the soul realized, "I don't need to transcend. I need to *return*."

That evening, the soul lit a candle and placed their bare feet on the floor. Not just to relax ~ but to *listen downward*. They spoke not to the stars, but to the bones.

Then, softly, they asked:

What part of me have I ignored that is holding everything together?
What root wants tending ~ not to blossom, but to simply stay strong?

Journal Prompts:

— What are the "roots" in my life that give me true
  strength?
— What foundational part of me needs nourishment?
— What ancestral, cultural, or personal wisdom am I ready
  to reclaim?

Sacred Actions: Prepare or eat something that comes from beneath the ground (like a root vegetable or herbal tea). With each bite or sip, silently thank what has grown in the dark to sustain you.

Symbolic Focus: The soles of the feet, the base of the spine, the gut.

Your Mantra for Today ~

"Not all medicine is upward. I grow strong by going deep."

January 18 - The Day of Pause and Purpose

A story of sacred stillness, intentional waiting, and the power of not moving until it's real

There once was a soul who rushed everything.

They rushed healing. Rushed answers. Rushed themselves out of discomfort before they could understand it. Waiting felt dangerous. Stillness, unbearable. They filled the silence with effort, with noise, with urgency.

But one day ~ this day ~ they stopped. Not because they wanted to, but because they couldn't keep going.

They sat at the edge of a long, flat field, nothing urgent ahead, nothing chasing behind. Just space. Just breath. And for the first time in a long while, they didn't try to make something happen.

They simply… paused.

At first, the mind begged for movement. *"Do something."* But then came a whisper from somewhere deeper:

"The pause *is* the purpose."

That line echoed through the stillness like a bell in snow.

It changed everything.

Today carries the energy of the number 18, reducing to 9 ~ the number of completion, wisdom, and deep inner truth. But this isn't the end of a cycle. It's the inhale before the next one. A sacred pause ~ not out of indecision, but integrity.

Under the grounded influence of Capricorn, the energy becomes practical: *"Don't rush because you're afraid. Wait because you're wise."*

The archetype of this day is The Timeless One ~ the soul who understands that rest is not a luxury, but a sacred responsibility. They hold space for clarity to rise naturally, not forcefully.

The symbols of this day are tender and potent:

— An hourglass, paused mid-turn

— Blue calcite, a stone of still calm and clear mind

— The Hanged Man, the tarot's master of perspective-through-pause

— A heron, standing still in water, waiting for the exact right moment

This day brings healing to those who associate worth with action, and who fear that waiting means wasting. If your survival was once tied to performance, this pause might feel threatening.

But today reminds you: *"You are not behind. You are aligning."*

And yet ~ in the soft quiet of this truth ~ a subtle curiosity stirs:

What if this pause is preparing me for something deeper than I imagined?

Later, the soul wrote not with urgency, but invitation:

- — Where am I trying to force clarity before it's ready?
- — What would it mean to trust the wisdom of waiting?
- — How would my body feel if I allowed rest without guilt?

No answers were needed Just space. Sometimes the question itself is the purpose.

Sacred Actions: Do one thing today ~ even for 5 minutes ~ *slowly*. Let it be inefficient. Let it be *felt*.

Trust what arises in the stillness.

Symbolic Focus: The breath, the solar plexus, the moments between thoughts.

Your Mantra for Today ~

"I pause not to escape. I pause to align."

January 19 - The Day of Soul Simplicity

A story of shedding the extra, trusting the essential, and returning to the quiet truth beneath it all

There once was a soul who tried to make things meaningful by making them bigger.

They thought depth required complexity. That their life had to be layered with grand ideas, intricate plans, and constant transformation to matter. Their bookshelf was overflowing, their calendar packed, their mind always searching for something more.

But one day ~ tired and full of noise ~ they did something unusual.

They stopped trying.

They sat on a bench with nothing but their breath, their hands, and the sound of leaves moving in the wind. No ritual. No journal. No purpose beyond *being there.*

And in that unadorned moment, something profound emerged.

"This," the soul realized, "is enough."

It wasn't boredom. It wasn't emptiness. It was *simplicity* ~ the kind that doesn't diminish meaning, but clarifies it.

The number 19 reduces to 1, marking a beginning ~ but this one is different. This isn't the first page of a new book. It's the rediscovery of the page that never needed editing. It's about returning to what matters most, and letting it be *enough*.

The Capricorn sun lends weight to this simplicity. It says: *"There is elegance in the essential. There is truth in what doesn't try too hard."*

The archetype of the day is The Quiet Keeper ~ the one who walks through life with gentle clarity, speaking little, seeing much, and knowing that sacred doesn't need to shout.

Today's symbols offer gentle guidance:

— A single stone, perfectly shaped by time

— White howlite, the stone of clarity and peaceful presence

— The Four of Pentacles, not hoarding, but cherishing what's truly yours

— A sparrow, small and unnoticed by many ~ yet steady, resourceful, true

This day offers healing for those who have over-complicated their own wisdom. For those who fear they aren't doing enough ~ and therefore fear they *aren't enough*.

"You are not here to impress," the day says. "You are here to be real."

And just as the soul began to relax into that truth, a quiet question arose ~ one too simple to ignore:

What if the clarity I seek is waiting beneath everything I've added on top of it?

Later that afternoon, the soul made tea and chose not to scroll, not to read, not to fix. They sat in silence and watched steam rise. That was it.

Being honest with yourself, ask:

— What would my life look like with 30% less noise?
— What truth do I already know ~ that doesn't need more explanation?
— What can I release today, not from pressure, but from peace?

The pen moved slowly. No rush. No push. Only presence.

Sacred Actions: Choose one thing to simplify today ~ a thought, a schedule block, a routine. Let it go. Breathe. Witness what returns in its place.

Symbolic Focus: The breath, the space between activities, the uncluttered moment.

Your Mantra for Today ~

"Simplicity is not emptiness. It is clarity."

January 20 - The Day of Embodied Awareness

A story of sensing your truth, returning to your body, and realizing the wisdom already living in your skin

There once was a soul who lived mostly in their head.

They thought their way through everything ~ feelings, decisions, even relationships. They were clever, capable, and often praised for their insight. But no matter how much they *knew*, something felt missing.

Their body had become a tool. A vehicle. A thing they managed rather than lived in. Then, one quiet morning, the soul was asked a strange question by someone who loved them:

"But where do you *feel* that?"

The soul paused ~ confused. Feel it? They hadn't thought to ask their body anything.

Later, alone, the soul lay flat on the ground. No cushion. No analysis. Just gravity. Breath. A moment of surrender.

And something began to rise ~ not a thought, but a sensation. A heaviness in the chest. A warmth in the belly. A knowing in the spine.

"Oh," the soul whispered. "There is a truth in me that doesn't speak in words."

Today carries the number 20, which reduces to 2 ~ the number of harmony, intuition, and relational wisdom. But this 2 isn't external. It's the sacred relationship between *you and your body*. You and your felt experience.

Under Capricorn's influence, this becomes embodied wisdom ~ not mystical escape, but sacred grounding. It's about *being in the body as an act of spiritual clarity*.

The archetype of the day is The Embodied Mystic ~ one who knows that presence is a sacred practice, and that no amount of intellect can replace what the breath already knows.

Today's symbols are rooted in the somatic:

— A body traced with light, energy flowing from foot to crown

— Carnelian, stone of vitality, warmth, and physical awareness

— The Queen of Cups, emotionally attuned and fully present

— A cat, aware of every step, every pause, every breath ~ no effort

This day offers healing for those who've been disconnected from their body ~ by trauma, by culture, by speed. For those who once had to leave their bodies to feel safe, and now long to come home to them.

"You don't have to figure it out today," the body says. "You only have to *feel it.*"

And as the soul lay still, a question shimmered beneath the skin:

If I trusted the sensations in my body as much as I trust my thoughts... what would I finally understand?

Later, the soul moved slowly through their space ~ barefoot, with intention. They sat, not in posture, but in comfort. They touched their own arms gently, as if saying: *"I see you. I live here. Thank you."*

And Being honest with yourself, ask:

— Where do I hold tension ~ and what might that tension be saying?

— How can I let my body guide one small decision today?

— What happens when I stop overriding what I feel?

No diagnosis. No dissection. Just awareness ~ honest, embodied, whole.

Sacred Actions: Place one hand over your heart and one on your belly. Breathe slowly. Ask aloud:

"What are you telling me that I haven't yet heard?"

Listen without needing to fix.

Symbolic Focus: The breath in the belly, the heart center, the soles of the feet.

Your Mantra for Today ~

"I live in my body. I trust what it knows."

January 21 - The Day of Ancestral Echoes

A story of remembering where you come from, reclaiming what you carry, and hearing the voices that live in your blood

There once was a soul who felt like a mystery to themselves.

They had lived many chapters ~ changed, evolved, transformed. But sometimes, in the quiet, they felt a longing they couldn't name.

A homesickness with no map. A grief that didn't belong to anything they could point to.

One day, while sitting alone beneath an old tree, the soul leaned back, closed their eyes ~ and felt it.

A rhythm. A breath not their own. A presence like wind through stone.

And then… a whisper. Not in words, but in memory:

"You are not the beginning. You are the continuation."

The soul opened their eyes, and for a moment, the world shimmered ~ not with something new, but something *ancient*.

It wasn't just their life they were carrying. It was a lineage.

And suddenly, everything made more sense.

Today is guided by the number 21, which reduces to 3 ~ a number of communication, legacy, and shared truth. But today, it doesn't ask you to speak outwardly. It asks you to listen inwardly ~ to the voices behind the veil.

Under Capricorn's slow and steady wisdom, this day becomes ancestral ground. You are invited to explore not only who you are, but *who shaped the soil from which you grow.*

The archetype of the day is The Echo Bearer ~ one who listens beyond time, who hears in dreams, and who turns inherited pain into purpose.

The symbols surrounding this day hum with ancient resonance:

— A drumbeat, low and slow, like a heartbeat across generations

— Black kyanite, the stone of energetic cord-cutting and spiritual lineage

— The Six of Cups, memory passed through emotion and sensation

— A raven, messenger between worlds, witness of shadow and wisdom

This day offers healing to those who carry wounds that didn't begin with them. If your body aches with unnamed grief, or your voice trembles without knowing why, today reminds you:

"You are not broken. You are bearing the echoes. And you get to respond." And somewhere inside, a tender curiosity rises:

If I could meet the ones who came before me ~ the gentle ones, the hurt ones, the fierce ones ~ what would they want me to know about being here, now, as me?

Later that day, the soul lit a small fire ~ maybe a candle, maybe something older ~ and wrote a simple letter.

Not to anyone living. But to the line of souls who stood behind them.

Being honest with yourself, ask:

— What parts of my life feel like echoes ~ familiar, but not mine?

— What strengths have I inherited that I never gave myself credit?

— What stories am I ready to end ~ and which ones am I ready to continue with intention?

Sacred Actions: Light a candle and say aloud:

"To those who came before me ~ I see you. I carry you. I choose with awareness now."

Let that be the ritual.

Symbolic Focus: The back of the heart, the spine, the soles of the feet.

Your Mantra for Today ~

"I am not alone in this becoming. I walk with those who walked before me."

January 22 - The Day of Deep Rest

A story of sacred surrender, nervous system healing, and the power of stopping without guilt

There once was a soul who kept going.

Even when they were tired. Even when their body whispered. Even when their spirit begged. They kept going ~ out of habit, fear, duty. They had been taught that to rest was to fall behind. That stopping meant weakness. That slowing down was something you had to earn.

But on this day ~ worn, quiet, and on the edge of something unseen ~ the soul stopped.

Not because they finally finished everything. Not because it was the weekend. Not because they had permission.

They stopped because their *body* asked. Because their *breath* fractured. Because they couldn't go one step further without breaking in half.

So they lay down. On the floor. On the earth. On the truth.

And in that moment ~ in the surrender ~ came the message they'd been running toward all along:

"You do not have to do more to be more."

That sentence wrapped around their bones like a soft blanket. Their breath deepened. Their chest stopped bracing. Their jaw released.

They did not fall asleep. They fell into being.

Today is guided by the number 22, a master number of foundation, peace, and divine architecture. But the foundation this day asks for is *rest*. It says: *What you build will only last if you yourself are whole.*

Under Capricorn's anchored energy, this becomes less about escape and more about embodiment. Today, rest isn't avoidance ~ it's *integration*.

The archetype of the day is The Rest Weaver ~ one who stitches space between each heartbeat, who knows that silence is not empty, but holy.

Symbols for this day ask for nothing but awareness:

— A bed of moss, undisturbed

— Lepidolite, a crystal for nervous system regulation and emotional reset

— The Four of Swords, sacred rest after sacred battle

— A sloth, not slow from laziness, but deeply attuned to rhythm

This day offers healing for those who feel unsafe when they stop. For those whose trauma taught them that stillness was dangerous. That rest would be punished, or seen as failure.

"You are not lazy," the day whispers. "You are living in a body that deserves peace."

And just as the soul softened into that knowing, a question shimmered through the quiet like stars breaking through fog:

What part of me is still fighting for permission to pause ~ when what I really need is a full surrender into rest?

Later, the soul turned off their alarm. They closed extra tabs. They chose not to respond. They didn't "earn" the break. They *honored* it.

Being honest with yourself, ask:

— What happens in me when I allow deep rest ~ not just physically, but emotionally?

— Where am I still holding tension because I feel I haven't done enough?

— What does "rest" mean to my spirit, beyond sleep?

There was no productivity. But there was peace. And peace ~ finally ~ was enough.

Sacred Actions: Cancel or soften one thing in your day. Replace it with silence, warmth, stillness, or solitude. Let that be your medicine.

Symbolic Focus: The vagus nerve, the back of the neck, the breath just before sleep.

Your Mantra for Today ~

"Rest is not a luxury. It is a return to myself."

January 23 - The Day of Quiet Courage

A story of subtle bravery, invisible battles, and the strength to stay true without needing to be loud

There once was a soul who believed courage had to look a certain way.

Bold. Loud. Defiant. Daring. They imagined warriors with swords, voices raised, flags planted.

So when they trembled through a conversation, or whispered a boundary, or took one small step forward through fear, they didn't call it courage. They called it *barely getting through*.

But on this day ~ cool, tender, honest ~ the soul looked back. Really looked.

They saw the moments when they chose truth over silence. When they stayed present in discomfort. When they got up after being undone.

And suddenly, they saw it differently.

"That wasn't survival," the soul realized. "That was courage. Quiet, sacred courage."

The number 23 reduces to 5 ~ the number of movement, change, and bravery through action. But today, it doesn't ask you to leap. It asks you to recognize how far you've already come ~ especially when no one was watching.

Under the enduring Capricorn sun, this energy becomes grounded. Practical. It says: *"Bravery is not about volume. It's about alignment."*

The archetype of the day is The Subtle Warrior ~ the one who walks into the room of their own shame and sits calmly, saying *"I'm still here."* The one whose strength is not in their shout, but in their quiet refusal to abandon themselves.

Today's symbols hum below the surface:

— A swan, graceful but strong, gliding through current

— Smoky quartz, the crystal of grounded resilience and transmutation

— The Nine of Wands, holding the line after a long journey

— A stone in the river, not budging, not sinking ~ simply *there*

This day offers healing to those who have discredited their strength because it didn't look like someone else's. For those who equated bravery with performance, and missed their own heroism in the still moments.

"You were brave," the day whispers, "even when all you did was *not give up*."

And as that truth rooted itself, a gentle question stirred in the soul like a ripple:

What acts of quiet courage have I not yet honored in myself ~ simply because they didn't look dramatic enough?

Later, the soul wrote a letter. Not to someone else. To themselves ~ the version who kept going when they wanted to quit. The version who showed up without applause. The version who whispered, *"I can try again tomorrow."*

Being honest with yourself, ask:

— What moments of my life deserve to be called courageous?

— What quiet bravery do I carry that no one else sees ~ but that I live through every day?

— How can I begin to honor those parts of myself now?

They didn't cry from sadness. They cried from recognition. From seeing the truth in their own reflection.

Sacred Actions: Say aloud to yourself in a mirror or photograph:

"I see how brave you've been."

And then name one thing ~ just one ~ that proves it.

Symbolic Focus: The diaphragm, the inner thighs, the hands gently curled in rest.

Your Mantra for Today ~

"My courage doesn't shout. It stays."

January 24 - The Day of Subtle Trust

A story of quiet surrender, sensing without proof, and learning to move before you know the whole path

There once was a soul who only trusted when the signs were clear.

They needed confirmations ~ green lights, clear maps, someone to say *"yes, go now."* Uncertainty made them hesitate. Fog made them freeze. If they couldn't see where the step led, they didn't take it.

But one day ~ mist thick over the hills, the sky unsure ~ the soul stood at the edge of something unnamed. No sign. No voice. No guarantee.

Only a feeling. A hum. A slight shift in the air that whispered:

"It's time."

The soul resisted. Waited for logic. Waited for clarity. It didn't come. Instead came a deeper voice ~ not from above, but from within:

"Can you trust this without needing to understand it yet?"

That was the invitation. Not to leap recklessly. But to *lean gently.*

Today carries the number 24, which reduces to 6 ~ the number of trust, inner knowing, and emotional balance. But today isn't about blind faith. It's about subtle trust ~ the kind that says, *"I don't have to see it all to begin."*

Under Capricorn's grounded guidance, this energy takes form as embodied intuition. You're not asked to believe in fantasies. You're asked to honor the quiet *yes* in your chest ~ even if it doesn't come with proof.

The archetype of the day is The Mist-Walker ~ the soul who moves with patience through uncertainty, knowing that some paths must be felt, not seen.

Today's symbols are soft but sure:

— A single lantern, lit but not blinding, guiding one step at a time

— Moonstone, for intuitive flow and emotional navigation

— The Two of Swords, a crossroads without pressure

— A fox, quiet-footed and alert, moving through unknown terrain with grace

This day offers healing to those who were punished for "just knowing," or whose inner compass was questioned so often they stopped using it. If trauma taught you to wait for safety in others instead of sensing it in yourself, this day says:

"You can trust the quiet inside you. It has been right before."

And just as the soul began to soften, a whisper of wonder rose:

What would change in my life if I trusted my gentle nudges more than my fear of being wrong?

That evening, the soul took a single step ~ not a big one, not symbolic, just *honest*. They moved a book. Texted a friend. Chose one thing that felt quietly right.

Being honest with yourself, ask:

— Where in my life do I wait too long for external confirmation?

— What do I already sense ~ but keep ignoring?

— What's one small thing I could do today as an act of self-trust?

They didn't need full clarity.

Just enough to begin.

Sacred Actions: Choose something that has been tugging at you ~ softly, quietly. Act on it, even in the smallest way. Let that be enough.

Symbolic Focus: The soles of the feet, the forehead, the gut center.

Your Mantra for Today ~

"I do not need all the answers. I only need to trust what I know right now."

January 25 - The Day of Steady Becoming

A story of patient unfolding, honoring the pace of growth, and trusting that slow doesn't mean stuck

There once was a soul who always felt behind.

Behind in healing. Behind in purpose. Behind in life.

They watched others bloom while they were still planting. They compared timelines, achievements, even emotions ~ wondering why their growth felt so… slow.

One day, walking past a winter garden, they noticed a patch of bare soil. A handwritten sign poked from the ground:

"Caution: Growth in Progress."

There was nothing visible. No sprouts. No color.

But something in those words stopped the soul completely.

They knelt beside the earth and laid a hand on the cold ground. There was no movement. No confirmation.

And yet ~ the moment held a kind of truth they hadn't allowed themselves to believe until now:

"Just because it's quiet doesn't mean it's not happening."

A warmth spread through their body. The pressure lifted.

They didn't need to bloom today. They only needed to become ~ slowly, truly, fully.

Today carries the number 25, which reduces to 7 ~ the number of inner wisdom, spiritual timing, and depth over speed. It invites you to let go of urgency and live in your *own* rhythm.

The Capricorn sun continues to offer steady ground. This isn't a day for leaps. It's a day for trusting the gentle slope of your becoming.

The archetype of the day is The Patient Grower ~ one who doesn't push the seed to rise, but tends the soil, waters with love, and knows that all real transformation takes time.

Today's symbols are simple but sacred:

— A seedling beneath soil, unseen but alive

— Moss agate, for slow integration and stability

— The Knight of Pentacles, devoted, methodical, enduring

— A turtle, moving without rush, arriving with certainty

This day offers healing for those who feel they should be further along. If you've equated fast with successful, or internalized urgency as a virtue, today says:

"You are not late. You are ripening."

And right there, as the soul absorbed that truth, a quiet question took root:

What might begin to bloom in me if I stopped forcing my pace and started trusting it instead?

Later, the soul lit a small candle ~ not to celebrate arrival, but to honor process.

They sat with their journal and wrote:

— What parts of me are growing invisibly right now?

— Where have I pressured myself to rush when what I really needed was more time?

— What does steady, soul-paced becoming feel like in my body today?

The answers were slow. But they came. And they came kindly.

Sacred Actions: Choose one thing in your day to slow down ~ intentionally. Let the slowness become its own sacred practice. Breathe into the pauses.

Symbolic Focus: The back body, the lower spine, the breath in the hips.

Your Mantra for Today ~ *"I become at the pace of truth. I do not rush the sacred."*

January 26 - The Day of Devoted Presence

A story of sacred attention, soul-level focus, and showing up fully for what matters most

There once was a soul who did everything ~ but felt almost nothing.

Their days were full, their lists checked off, their schedule overflowing. Yet when they lay down at night, they felt scattered. Numb.
Like they were living beside their life rather than *in* it.

Then one day, sitting at the kitchen table with a hot drink cooling in their hands, the soul noticed… they couldn't remember taking a single conscious sip.

The warmth. The taste. The quiet. All of it had passed through them, untouched.

They put the cup down. Closed their eyes. And whispered:

"I want to be here. For *this*."

From that small prayer, something opened. Not a grand awakening ~ just a gentle re-entry. A sacred click of awareness into alignment.

"Devotion," they realized, "is not about what you do. It's about how fully you do it."

Today carries the number 26, which reduces to 8 ~ a number of embodied power and focused energy. But the power today speaks in presence, not performance. In how you show up, not how much you do.

Under Capricorn's steady light, this presence becomes sacred structure. It says: *"You don't need to multitask your way through your life. You need to land in it ~ one breath at a time."*

The archetype of the day is The Flame Tender ~ the one who stays near the fire, who tends the ordinary until it becomes holy, who knows that devotion is not in grand acts, but in quiet constancy.

Today's symbols invite grounding and grace:

— A burning hearth, glowing and sustained

— Red jasper, for energy, consistency, and rooted focus

— The Eight of Pentacles, devotion to the task, the craft, the care

— A bee, not rushing, but returning ~ again and again ~ to the same flower

This day offers healing for those who feel fragmented ~ who do many things but feel connected to none. For those whose survival once depended on doing, producing, achieving ~ and who now long for *presence over pressure*.

"Your life is not waiting for you somewhere else," the day whispers. "It's right here. In this moment. In this breath."

And as the soul leaned into that knowing, a quiet question surfaced like steam from a just-poured cup:

What part of my life is asking for my full attention ~ not my effort, just my presence?

Later, the soul returned to that same drink ~ now warm again. This time, they held it with both hands. Felt the heat. Took a breath. And drank *slowly.*

Being honest with yourself, ask:

— Where in my life am I showing up half-present?

— What rituals ~ small or sacred ~ want more of my attention?

— What happens when I stop rushing through the moments meant to nourish me?

They didn't make a vow. They made a choice ~ to return, again and again, to *here.*

Sacred Actions: Pick one daily task ~ eating, bathing, folding clothes ~ and do it *with devotion.* No distractions. No rush. Let it become a meditation.

Symbolic Focus: The fingertips, the heart space, the space behind the eyes.

Your Mantra for Today ~

"I devote myself to this moment. That is enough."

January 27 - The Day of Inner Sanctuary

A story of sacred retreat, creating safety within, and the quiet shelter that's been waiting inside you all along

There once was a soul who searched everywhere for peace.

They tried new places, new people, new routines. They rearranged their home, repainted their walls, played calming sounds. But the restlessness followed.

No matter where they went, their mind came with them. Their nervous system stayed alert. Their heart kept bracing for something they couldn't name.

One rainy afternoon, with nowhere to be and nothing urgent to do, the soul sat in silence. Just… sat. No incense. No music. No plan.

They closed their eyes and imagined a space. Not external. Not imagined. *Felt.*

It was warm. Quiet. Womb-like. A place where nothing was asked of them. Where breath was enough. Where being was welcomed without condition.

And the soul heard, from within:

"This is your sanctuary. You do not need to find it. You need to return."

Today is guided by the number 27, which reduces to 9 ~ the number of integration, wisdom, and inward completion. It invites you to step back from the outer noise and remember that your truest refuge isn't found ~ it's *built within*.

Under Capricorn's grounded architecture, this sanctuary becomes more than a metaphor. It becomes embodied. Rooted. Real.

You are invited to build a relationship with your inner shelter ~ the place you carry no matter what life throws your way.

The archetype of the day is The Sanctuary Keeper ~ the one who tends to their inner landscape with care, who creates space for rest, grief, reflection, and quiet joy.

Today's symbols evoke warmth and return:

— A hearth hidden deep within a cave

— Amethyst, for protection, peace, and inner vision

— The Four of Cups, the soul's retreat from overwhelm into meaningful stillness

— A turtle, withdrawing not in fear, but in self-trust

This day offers healing for those whose lives have been lived in reaction ~ always adapting, surviving, adjusting. If safety was something you had to search for outside yourself, today says:

"There is a home within you that cannot be taken."

And in that stillness, a gentle question appears like a doorway half-open:

What kind of inner sanctuary would I build for myself ~ if I truly believed I was worthy of peace?

Later, the soul gathered a few items ~ a soft scarf, a candle, a journal ~ and created a small space. Not fancy. Not curated. Just *intentional.*

They sat in that space and wrote:

— What does "safety" feel like in my body? When have I felt it?

— What parts of me still believe I must earn peace?

— How can I make contact with my inner sanctuary today ~ even for just five minutes?

No answers needed. The sanctuary did not demand them. It only asked: *Come in. Rest.*

Sacred Actions: Designate a corner of your day as sanctuary ~ a moment, a breath, a chair, a pause. Protect it as if it were a temple.

Symbolic Focus: The pelvic bowl, the lower belly, the center of the chest.

Your Mantra for Today ~

"My peace lives inside me. I return to it now."

January 28 - The Day of Quiet Reflection

A story of gentle truth-telling, soulful mirroring, and the courage to see without judgment

There once was a soul who was always moving ~ mind first.

They reflected often… but mostly in motion. They analyzed while walking, processed while talking, reviewed while planning. Their reflections were fast, sharp, efficient.

But one day, something shifted.

They sat by a window with a journal on their lap and nothing to say. The light hit the glass just right, and their reflection appeared ~ soft, unguarded, real.

No posing. No thinking. Just being.

They stared at themselves in the quiet and saw not a problem to solve, but a presence to meet.

Not a story. A soul.

"This is what it means to reflect," they thought. "Not to dissect. But to witness."

And suddenly, the silence between thoughts became sacred.

Today is held by the number 28, which reduces to 1 ~ the number of new beginnings. But this isn't a beginning built on urgency. It's a beginning born from clarity. A start that comes *after* deep seeing.

Under Capricorn's structure, this becomes an act of devotion ~ not to productivity, but to *truth*. You are invited to reflect today not to fix, but to face. Gently. Honestly. With reverence.

The archetype of the day is The Soul Mirror ~ the one who reflects without distortion, who learns to hold their own gaze, who becomes intimate with their becoming.

Today's symbols feel still, luminous, and open:

— A still lake, undisturbed, reflecting the whole sky

— Selenite, for clarity, spiritual cleansing, and pure reflection

— The Page of Swords, curious, observant, on the threshold of deeper insight

— A white owl, watching from a high branch, seeing everything in silence

This day offers healing for those who fear what they'll find when they stop. If you've equated self-reflection with shame, overthinking, or analysis paralysis ~ today says:

"You don't have to judge what you see. You only have to *gently meet it.*"

And as you soften into that meeting, a curiosity arises like ripples on still water:

What truths might come into view if I looked at myself not with critique, but with curiosity and compassion?

Later, the soul sat with their reflection ~ in a mirror, a photo, a journal page ~ and asked no questions. They simply *looked*, breathed, and let what wanted to rise... rise.

Being honest with yourself, ask:

— What do I see when I look at myself slowly, without agenda?

— What feels tender in me today ~ not broken, but vulnerable?

— What am I beginning to understand now that I didn't before?

No fixing. No sorting. Just presence.

Sacred Actions: Find a reflective surface ~ mirror, water, even a window at dusk ~ and sit with it for 3 minutes. Breathe. Look. Say:

"I see you. I'm here."

Symbolic Focus: The eyes, the breath, the space between the heartbeats.

Your Mantra for Today ~

"I witness myself with kindness. That is enough."

January 29 - The Day of Sacred Timing

A story of trust in the unfolding, divine pace, and the release of "when" in favor of "why now"

There once was a soul obsessed with timing.

They checked the clock, the calendar, the milestones. Compared their path to others. Measured everything in *"by now"* and *"not yet."*

They feared missing their moment. They feared being too late. They feared being the only one still waiting.

One evening, watching the last rays of sun stretch across a wall, the soul heard something surprising ~ not a voice, but a feeling:

"You have never missed your moment. You *are* the moment."

They sat with that.

All the pressure… softened. All the urgency… stilled.

Because something deeper began to speak ~ the rhythm of their own life, beating quietly beneath all expectations.

Today carries the number 29, which reduces to 11, then 2 ~ a master number wrapped in wisdom, intuition, and alignment. But the kind of alignment that doesn't happen on a timer.

It happens when *you* are ready ~ and not a moment before.

Capricorn's influence today creates a container. A structure for trust. It says: *"This isn't about delay. This is about preparation."*

The archetype of the day is The Timekeeper of the Soul ~ the one who knows that the universe doesn't rush truth. Who honors cycles, seasons, and the mystery of perfect arrival.

Today's symbols tick with quiet faith:

— A clock with no hands, surrounded by stars

— Divine timing cards, drawn in silence and trust

— Rutilated quartz, crystal of alignment and destiny

— A cicada, underground for years, emerging only when fully ready

This day offers healing for those who have shamed themselves for being "behind." For those who think they should've figured it out, done it, healed it… sooner.

"You're not late," the day says. "You're right on time for *your* life."

And in that surrender, a sacred wonder blooms:

If I let go of the pressure of "when," what doors might open to "why now?"

Later, the soul sat without their schedule. Just themselves and the   sky.
And slowly, they felt it ~ a rhythm that didn't come from their planner, but their pulse.

Being honest with yourself, ask:

— What if my timing is not wrong ~ just not aligned with what I thought I needed?

— What have I been rushing that actually needs space to unfold?

— Where is patience actually protecting something sacred in me?

And then, the words came:

"I trust that I'm right where I'm meant to be ~ even if I can't see why yet."

Sacred Actions: Take one task or goal you've been pressuring yourself over and consciously loosen your grip. Say aloud:

Symbolic Focus: The chest cavity, the fingertips, the breath during exhale.

Your Mantra for Today ~

"I am not behind. I am becoming, in sacred time."

January 30 - The Day of Honest Integration

A story of gathering the pieces, embracing contradictions, and becoming whole without needing to be perfect

There once was a soul who kept trying to "figure it all out."

They sought the clean narrative ~ the tidy timeline, the resolved ending, the one clear version of self they could finally settle into.

But every time they thought they had it ~ a new layer emerged. A contradiction surfaced. A past part returned. They began to wonder if they'd ever *arrive*.

One day, sitting in the quiet after a long cry, the soul whispered:

"I don't know who I am right now."

And then... something surprising answered back.

Not in words ~ but in a feeling:

"That's okay. You're not *one* thing. You're all of it."

The shame lifted. The pressure softened. They weren't broken or lost ~ they were *becoming integrated.*

Today holds the number 30, which reduces to 3 ~ the number of self-expression, reflection, and creative wholeness. But this isn't about external creation ~ it's about the internal weaving together of everything you are.

Capricorn, in its final days, brings discipline to the process of inner fusion. It says: *"You don't need to erase your past selves. You need to bring them home."*

The archetype of the day is The Inner Weaver ~ one who threads together fragments, honors contradictions, and knows that wisdom isn't about consistency ~ it's about *coherence.*

Today's symbols feel humble and whole:

— A woven tapestry, imperfect but complete

— Labradorite, for embracing paradox and integrating shadow

— The Temperance card, mixing what was once separate into sacred blend

— A spider, weaving patiently from all directions ~ never needing symmetry to create beauty

This day offers healing for those who have judged themselves for being inconsistent, messy, "too much" or "too scattered." It says:

"You are not a puzzle missing pieces. You are a mosaic in progress ~ and every piece matters."

And in that grace, a question floats up like a final piece clicking gently into place:

What if my healing doesn't make me simpler... it makes me more whole?

Later, the soul opened an old notebook. Pages filled with dreams, doubts, and drafts of selves they once thought they had to become.

Instead of shame, they smiled. *"Every version of me got me here."*

Being honest with yourself, ask:

— What parts of me have I disowned ~ and why?

— What beliefs or identities am I trying to "fix" that actually just want to be seen?

— How can I live as a more complete ~ not cleaner ~ version of myself?

They closed the notebook, not with answers, but with acceptance.

Sacred Actions: Pick one part of yourself you usually reject ~ a fear, a memory, a behavior ~ and write it a letter that begins:

"Thank you for trying to protect me. I see you now."

Symbolic Focus: The solar plexus, the shoulders, the inner landscape behind the heart.

Your Mantra for Today ~

"I gather every part of me. I do not need to be simple to be whole."

January 31 - The Day of Soul Embers

A story of lingering warmth, quiet endurance, and the fire that still burns beneath the ashes

There once was a soul who feared they had lost their spark.

Not long ago, they burned with passion, purpose, vision ~ but lately, the fire felt dim. Their motivation flickered. Their voice wavered. The heat that once fueled them seemed to have cooled into something quieter… harder to define.

They thought they were fading.

But one night, sitting beside a dying fire, they watched the last coals pulse gently in the dark ~ small, quiet, steady.

And in that red glow, they saw something they had forgotten:

"The fire isn't gone. It's just become an ember."

That ember didn't shout. It didn't dance. But it didn't die either.

It waited.

It breathed.

It knew its time would come again.

Today, the final day of January, holds the number 31, which reduces to 4 ~ the number of foundation, sustainability, and long-term strength. This day invites you to honor the parts of your soul that burn slowly… but never go out.

Under the final degree of Capricorn, the message is clear: What endures is not always what shines.

The archetype of the day is The Ember Keeper ~ one who tends to their inner flame with patience, who protects the quiet fire through seasons of rest, and who knows that heat is not always visible, but always alive.

The symbols of the day carry warmth, endurance, and stillness:

— A coal nestled in ash, glowing faintly in the dark

— Fire agate, a stone of rekindling, inner flame, and quiet strength

— The Hermit card, walking alone not to escape, but to preserve

— A red fox, curled in its den, conserving energy for the moment that matters

This day brings healing for those who think they've lost their passion, purpose, or drive. For those in burnout. For those waiting for "it" to come back.

"You have not lost your fire," the day says. "You have simply entered the ember season. It is sacred."

And in that warmth, a flicker of wonder rises:

What if this low flame is not a weakness ~ but a wisdom I've never been taught to trust?

Later, the soul sat with a candle ~ not newly lit, but long burning ~ its flame small, yet unwavering.

They breathed with it. Matched its rhythm. And wrote:

— What fire still lives in me, even if it's no longer roaring?

— What do I need to protect while it quietly burns?

— What would it mean to trust that even the smallest flame can be enough?

They didn't try to spark something new. They simply stayed with the ember.

Sacred Actions: Sit with a literal or imagined ember today ~ a candle's core, a memory, a desire. Say:

"You are still with me. I will not let you go."

Symbolic Focus: The base of the spine, the gut, the breath during stillness.

Your Mantra for Today ~

"My fire does not need to be loud. It only needs to last."

January Reflection

Rooted in Stillness: Honoring What Has Begun Within

As January closes, resist the urge to measure.
Instead ~ listen. This month was not about achievement. It was about arrival.

The days you spent with these pages were an invitation to plant seeds.

— Not for immediate harvest ~ but for *deep rooting*.

— For small truths to settle beneath the surface.

— For your inner life to stretch, unseen but alive, beneath the frost of habit and expectation.

Before you enter February, pause and ask: What Has Taken Root?

Reflect on the stillness that shaped this month.

— What part of me has softened into presence this month?

— What truth have I begun to trust ~ even if I can't yet explain why?

— Which day or entry from January keeps echoing through me ~ and why?

— Have I let stillness become part of my rhythm… or am I still resisting the pause?

— What seed have I planted that no one else can see ~ but I can feel growing?

Seeded Wisdom to Carry Forward

Wholeness is not rushed. There is no prize for blooming early. In the sacred stillness of January, perhaps you discovered:

— How to listen before speaking

— How to hold yourself gently at the edge of a new year

— How to feel the difference between pressure and purpose

— How to begin… *without running*

Whatever emerged, even faintly ~ *honor it.*

Integration Practice

Create a ritual of quiet recognition.

Tonight or tomorrow morning, sit in stillness for 3 minutes.
No journaling. No fixing. Just presence.
Place one hand on your chest, one on your belly, and say
aloud:

"I have begun. And that is enough."

Then ask yourself:

*What one rhythm from January will I continue to carry ~ not because I
must, but because it brings me home to myself?*

Write that rhythm down. Keep it visible. Let it guide February,
quietly.

Closing Mantra for January

"I began in stillness. I am rooted in truth.

What grows next will come in its own time.

I trust the unseen. I honor the seed."

February 1 - The Day of Soul Invitation

A story of gentle emergence, quiet willingness, and the sacred yes that begins before the bloom

There once was a soul who thought awakening had to be dramatic.

That opening required lightning bolts, epiphanies, or an unmistakable sign.

They waited for the big moment. The cosmic "go." But instead, what arrived was something far quieter.

A breeze. A shift in light. An invitation ~ not from the sky, but from within.

It didn't demand. It didn't rush. It simply whispered:

"You are ready to begin ~ not with certainty, but with willingness."

And in that moment, the soul realized: Not all openings are loud. Some are a soft leaning toward the light.

Today begins with the number 1 ~ the number of beginnings, self-awareness, and choice. But this "1" doesn't ask for action yet. It offers a doorway. A threshold. A chance to say yes before knowing what comes next.

With Aquarius now leading the zodiac, the energy becomes lighter ~ airier ~ but still rooted in *truth*. You are invited into possibility. Into expansion. Into a new season of soul.

The archetype of the day is The Soul Initiate ~ the one who says yes not because they're fully ready, but because something inside them has already begun to move.

Today's symbols feel light, spacious, and open:

- A bud just beginning to unfurl, kissed by morning air
- Aquamarine, a stone of emotional flow and softened truth
- The Ace of Cups, the heart saying yes before the mind agrees
- A fawn, newly born, still trembling, but standing nonetheless

This day brings healing to those who think they must have everything figured out before they begin. For those who delay joy, love, or presence until they feel "worthy" or "prepared."

"You don't need to bloom to begin," the day whispers. "You only need to open enough for light to reach you."

And in that softness, a new kind of question emerges:

What is quietly inviting me forward ~ that I've been too cautious to answer?

Later, the soul sat in silence ~ not to decide anything, but to listen.
Not to plan, but to feel.

And slowly, with no drama, they said aloud:

"I am open to becoming."

Being honest with yourself, ask:

- What invitations have I been receiving ~ through dreams, nudges, emotions ~ that I've been afraid to accept?
- Where in my life am I being asked to soften, rather than sprint?
- What would it feel like to say yes ~ without needing all the details?

They folded the page and placed it near the window ~ an offering to the wind.

Sacred Actions: Say yes to something today ~ no matter how small. A thought. A feeling. A moment of clarity. Say:

"I welcome this. Even if I do not fully understand it."

Symbolic Focus: The heart center, the collarbones, the breath that leads into a sigh.

Your Mantra for Today ~

"I open, gently. That is enough."

February 2 - The Day of Subtle Awakening

A story of quiet emergence, tender noticing, and the shift that happens not with noise, but with presence

There once was a soul who thought awakening had to feel big.

A jolt. A revelation. A moment of undeniable transformation.

So they waited ~ eyes open, spirit braced ~ hoping for that life-altering sign.

But what came instead was much smaller.

A yawn that reached deeper than sleep. A deeper exhale. A sudden awareness of how tightly they'd been holding everything.

They looked around and saw things differently ~ not because the world had changed, but because they were beginning to soften into *seeing*.

It wasn't a spark. It was a thaw.

"This," the soul whispered, "is what it feels like to awaken without breaking."

February 2 holds the vibration of 2 ~ the number of harmony, intuition, and relational depth. Today, this energy isn't loud or expressive. It is deeply felt and barely seen. This is the realm of subtle shifts ~ the kind that change everything, slowly.

With Aquarius still offering lightness and breath, today becomes an invitation to notice the nearly invisible ~ the *pre-bloom*, the *pre-knowing*, the *pre-spring*. This is not arrival. This is *awakening in process.*

The archetype of the day is The Quiet Stirrer ~ the one who feels the turn in the soil before the seed breaks open, the one who senses truth before it takes form.

Symbols of the day arrive like whispers:

— A dew drop on the edge of a leaf, trembling in morning light

— Celestite, stone of soft clarity and gentle spiritual connection

— The High Priestess, keeper of what stirs just beneath the surface

— A butterfly cocoon, pulsing faintly, just before the stretch

This day brings healing for those who think their growth doesn't count because it isn't visible. For those who've confused stillness with stagnation. For those who awaken slowly and have mistaken that for delay.

"You are awakening," the day says, "even if no one sees it. Even if you don't fully feel it yet."

And in the pause between one breath and the next, a question hums in the quiet:

What am I slowly becoming that I haven't yet given myself credit for?

Later, the soul stepped outside and simply stood beneath the sky ~ not asking, not reaching, just *being*. And in that presence, they felt it:

A little more space in the lungs.

A little more truth in the bones.

A little more willingness to keep unfolding.

Being honest with yourself, ask:

— What has quietly shifted in me lately ~ even if it hasn't fully arrived?

— Where am I awakening gently, without labels or plans?

— What deserves to be acknowledged ~ even in its early, fragile form?

The pen moved slowly. But each word felt like a stretch into morning.

Sacred Actions: Pause three times today to simply *notice* your breath, your skin, your surroundings. Say silently:

"I feel the shift. I allow it."

Symbolic Focus: The third eye, the nape of the neck, the breath at the edge of waking.

Your Mantra for Today ~

"My awakening does not need to be loud. It only needs to be true."

February 3 - The Day of Gentle Reconnection

A story of circling back, soft repair, and the sacred act of meeting yourself ~ and others ~ where the heart still waits

There once was a soul who had drifted.

From themselves. From others. From the things that once brought joy.

It wasn't intentional. Life just… layered itself. Time passed. Silence widened. Distance became easier than closeness.

But one day, while folding laundry and humming an old song they hadn't heard in years, something stirred. A memory. A warmth. A *pull*.

The soul paused. Touched the fabric. Closed their eyes.

"You're still here," they whispered ~ not to the song, not to the memory, but to the part of themselves they hadn't spoken to in a long time.

And in that tiny, honest moment, a bridge began to rebuild. No grand reunion. Just a simple turning toward.

February 3 brings the energy of 3 ~ expression, communication, and connection. But today, the emphasis isn't on performance. It's on repair ~ the gentle act of returning to what matters, even after time or silence.

With Aquarius guiding the heart through air and thought, this reconnection is not dramatic. It's felt like a hand reaching across a small space. Not to demand, but to offer.

The archetype of the day is The Soft Rebuilder ~ the one who reopens closed doors, who returns to inner truths with humility, who makes space for grace in reconnection.

Today's symbols speak of warmth and reaching:

— A bridge of vines, growing slowly between two trees

— Rhodonite, for emotional healing, compassion, and rebalancing the heart

— The Six of Cups, returning with tenderness to something once known

— A pair of doves, sitting quietly near each other, no words needed

This day offers healing for those who feel shame around distance ~ from loved ones, from purpose, from self. For those who've thought, *"It's too late to come back."*

"You don't need the perfect words," the day whispers. "You only need the willingness to return."

And with that truth, a question forms like a knot gently loosening:

What or who am I quietly ready to reconnect with ~ even if just a little at a time?

Later, the soul picked up an old book. Or a forgotten project. Or texted someone they hadn't spoken to in months ~ not to fix the past, but to re-enter the present.

Being honest with yourself, ask:

— Where have I drifted from myself ~ and how might I return today?

— Who or what deserves a soft reaching out ~ not for closure, but for reconnection?

— What part of me have I been avoiding... that is still waiting with kindness?

They didn't make promises.

They made contact.

Sacred Actions: Choose one thread to gently pick up again ~ a person, a practice, a truth. Do it softly. No apology needed. Just return.

Symbolic Focus: The hands, the throat, the back of the heart.

Your Mantra for Today ~

"I return with gentleness. I am allowed to begin again."

February 4 - The Day of Inner Friendship

A story of self-companionship, quiet loyalty, and becoming someone you trust from the inside out

There once was a soul who was kind to others but cruel to themselves.

They forgave friends quickly, encouraged strangers with ease, and listened patiently to those in pain. But inside? Their own inner voice was sharp. Cold. Demanding.

They tried to silence it. To push past it. To ignore it.

But one day ~ while walking alone in early morning light ~ the soul imagined what it would be like to walk beside someone who loved them exactly as they were.

No fixing. No judgment. Just presence.

"What if that someone," they thought, "could be *me*?"

Something in their chest softened. And for the first time, they didn't try to *improve themselves*. They tried to *befriend themselves*.

February 4 carries the number 4 ~ the number of stability, foundations, and trust. Today it invites you to form that trust *within*, not through performance or perfection, but through inner companionship.

With Aquarius still shaping the air around you, the call is clear:

The most important connection you can tend today is the one between you… and you.

The archetype of the day is The Inner Ally ~ the one who shows up for themselves with the same devotion they offer others, who chooses loyalty to self not out of isolation, but out of love.

Today's symbols speak of gentle bonding:

— A woven bracelet, tied around a wrist by your own hands

— Rose quartz, the crystal of unconditional love and heart tenderness

— The Two of Cups, not as a romance ~ but as a mirror of soul meeting soul

— A dog, loyal without condition, present without demand

This day brings healing for those who have been taught they must be harsh to improve, critical to succeed, or unrelenting to survive. For those who feel exhausted by their own inner voice.

"You do not need to be your own enemy to grow," the day says.

"You can walk beside yourself now ~ and be kind."

And with that shift comes a deeper question:

What if I chose to befriend myself ~ not one day, but today? What might change?

Later, the soul made tea for one. But not out of loneliness ~ out of reverence.

They sat with themselves as they would with someone they loved ~ gently, slowly, without agenda.

Being honest with yourself, ask:

— What tone does my inner voice carry most often ~ and is it truly mine?

— What do I most need from myself today, and am I willing to offer it?

— If I treated myself as a trusted friend, how would I move through this moment?

There was no resolution. Just *relationship*.

Sacred Actions: Write yourself a short note as if you were your own best friend. Begin with:

"I see you. I'm here. I've got you."

Read it aloud. Let it settle.

Symbolic Focus: The inner chest, the wrists, the breath after self-forgiveness.

Your Mantra for Today ~

"I am learning to befriend myself. And that is everything."

February 5 - The Day of Soul Gentleness

A story of softening, surrendering the inner battle, and discovering the quiet power of being tender with yourself

There once was a soul who confused strength with sharpness.

They spoke to themselves in the tone they'd heard from others ~ critical, impatient, exacting. They believed that pushing harder would make them better. That self-compassion was weak. That gentleness meant giving up.

But one day, as they sat in the sunlight filtering through their window, something melted.

They weren't trying to change. They weren't trying to prove anything. They just... stopped.

And in that pause, they heard something new. Not a voice. A feeling. A warm breath of truth rising from inside:

"What if I don't need to fight myself to grow?"

It landed softly. Like light touching water.

February 5 holds the energy of 5 ~ a number of transformation, freedom, and internal movement. But today, the movement comes not through force ~ but through gentleness.

With Aquarius offering emotional clarity and forward-leaning breath, this day doesn't ask you to figure anything out. It asks you to *soften into what's already unfolding.*

The archetype of the day is The Soul Soother ~ the one who tends to their own hurt with presence instead of pressure, who learns that softness is not the opposite of strength ~ it's its *root.*

The symbols of the day invite calm and quiet strength:

— A feather resting on water, moving only with breath

— Pink calcite, a crystal of emotional healing and softened perception

— The Page of Cups, open-hearted, tentative, and full of new softness

— A cloud, drifting slowly but never stagnant ~ carried by trust

This day brings healing for those who carry invisible wounds from inner criticism. For those who learned to be "strong" by shutting down. For those who fear that if they go easy on themselves, they'll collapse.

"You don't need to fight to be worthy," the day whispers. "You are allowed to heal without hurting yourself first."

And then, almost shyly, a gentle curiosity rises:

What would shift if I treated myself today like someone in need of comfort ~ not correction?

Later, the soul wrapped themselves in a blanket ~ not because they were cold, but because they were ready to feel safe.

They didn't push themselves to perform.

They simply asked:

- — Where am I being too hard on myself right now?
- — What would gentleness look like today ~ in word, in action, in breath?
- — What part of me is waiting to be spoken to with softness?

No answers came quickly. But the asking was its own beginning.

Sacred Actions: When a harsh inner voice arises today, pause. Breathe. Then, in the softest tone you can find, whisper to yourself:

"You're doing the best you can. And that is enough."

Symbolic Focus: The shoulders, the chest, the breath during exhale.

Your Mantra for Today ~

"Gentleness is not weakness. It is my quiet strength."

February 6 - The Day of Emotional Honesty

A story of truth-telling, brave expression, and the healing that begins when you stop pretending everything is fine

There once was a soul who had become very good at saying "I'm okay."

Even when they weren't. Even when the storm inside was loud. Even when their eyes said more than their voice ever dared.

They didn't lie out of deceit ~ they lied out of protection. Out of habit. Out of fear that their truth would be too much, or worse ~ ignored.

But one evening, while sitting across from someone they trusted, the soul surprised themselves. Their guard dropped for just a moment, and the words came out:

"Actually… I'm not okay today."

The silence that followed wasn't awkward. It was sacred.

In that moment, something cracked ~ not brokenness, but *relief*. They had spoken. And they were still here.

February 6 carries the energy of 6 ~ the number of harmony, healing, and emotional balance. Today, that balance is not about "feeling good." It's about being *true*. About naming what's real so it can breathe.

Under Aquarius's open air, truth rises easily ~ if you let it. This is a day for *clear-hearted expression*, not confession for drama, but honesty for *liberation*.

The archetype of the day is The Truth Tender ~ the one who holds space for rawness, who speaks not to be heard but to be *whole*, who knows that honesty is a bridge back to the self.

Today's symbols carry clarity and courage:

— A window cracked open, letting fresh air into a heavy room

— Amazonite, stone of emotional truth and throat chakra healing

— The Queen of Swords, who cuts through confusion with compassion

— A songbird, singing not to perform ~ but because the song must be sung

This day brings healing for those who have been silenced ~ by others, or by their own survival instincts. For those who carry layers of unspoken grief, anger, tenderness, or longing.

"You don't have to say it perfectly," the day whispers. "You only have to say it truthfully."

And as the soul breathed into that space, a powerful question rose like a tide:

What truth have I been holding back ~ not because it's unworthy, but because I thought I wasn't allowed to speak it?

Later, the soul sat with their journal, or voice memo app, or a trusted friend ~ and said what needed saying. Not the polished version. Just the real one.

Being honest with yourself, ask:

— What emotion am I truly feeling underneath my performance today?

— What truth wants to rise in me ~ even if it shakes as it speaks?

— How would it feel to express without apologizing or diluting?

No audience. No edits. Just release.

Sacred Actions: Say one thing aloud today ~ to yourself or another ~ that you've been keeping inside. Let your tone be kind. Let your voice be yours.

Symbolic Focus: The throat, the jaw, the heart behind the voice.

Your Mantra for Today ~

"I speak from truth. Even softly, it sets me free."

February 7 - The Day of Inner Listening

A story of tuning inward, quiet truths, and remembering that wisdom often whispers before it speaks

There once was a soul who searched everywhere for guidance.

They read books. Asked mentors. Pulled cards. Watched for signs.
And while wisdom came, it always felt *just outside* their grasp ~ as if they were circling something they couldn't quite touch.

Then one morning, in a moment of frustration, the soul stopped searching and sat in silence. Not to meditate. Not to fix. Just to *be still*.

And something surprising happened.

Not a voice. Not a vision. Just a sense. A subtle nudge in the ribs. A knowing that had *always* been there.

"You were listening outward," it said. "But your soul speaks *inwardly*."

The soul blinked. Then smiled. They hadn't been missing the message. They'd just been too loud to hear it.

February 7 carries the energy of 7 ~ a number of spiritual depth, inner awareness, and sacred solitude. It's a day that invites you to *lower the volume of the world* so you can finally hear what's already alive inside you.

With Aquarius still lending clarity through breath and thought, today doesn't push for answers. It invites *reception*. A willingness to listen ~ not for noise, but for nuance.

The archetype of the day is The Soul Listener ~ the one who learns that silence is not empty, and that the truest wisdom is usually soft, spacious, and just beneath the surface.

Today's symbols are hushed, but resonant:

— A shell held to the ear, echoing something vast

— Blue lace agate, a crystal of peaceful perception and inward hearing

— The Hermit, seeking not escape but quiet illumination

— A white deer, alert and calm, ears turned to the unseen

This day brings healing for those who've lost touch with their inner compass ~ who've relied so long on external validation that their own voice feels foreign.

"You are not directionless," the day whispers. "You are just overdue for stillness."

And in that pause, a soft question rises like a feather drifting into awareness:

What wisdom inside me have I been asking others to speak aloud?

Later, the soul found a small corner ~ maybe outside, maybe by a window ~ and sat. No headphones. No scroll. Just breath. Just attention.

Being honest with yourself, ask:

— When was the last time I listened to myself without interruption?

— What thoughts keep repeating ~ not to torment me, but to be heard?

— If my body could speak right now… what would it say?

There were no revelations. Just recognition. And that was enough.

Sacred Actions: Turn off all external sound for five minutes today. Sit in silence. Then ask aloud:

"What do I need to hear that only I can tell myself?"

Wait. Listen. Trust the quiet.

Symbolic Focus: The ears, the solar plexus, the space behind the sternum.

Your Mantra for Today ~

"I turn inward. My soul has something to say."

February 8 - The Day of Soft Boundaries

A story of sacred limits, gentle protection, and learning that saying no can be an act of deep love

There once was a soul who gave too much ~ not because they didn't matter, but because they *forgot they did*.

They said yes when they meant maybe. They offered energy they didn't have. They held space for others while abandoning their own needs.

For a while, it felt like love. Until the exhaustion came. The resentment. The quiet ache of being invisible in rooms they kept lighting from within.

One afternoon, as the soul stood near the ocean, they watched the tide pull back ~ not in rejection, but in rhythm.

The sea didn't apologize for its retreat. It returned because it left. It could offer waves because it knew when to rest.

"That," the soul thought, "is what my boundaries could feel like ~ not walls, but tides."

February 8 holds the energy of 8 ~ the number of power, self-worth, and embodied authority. Today, it teaches that boundaries are not barriers. They are bridges to *sustainable connection*.

With Aquarius still holding the emotional air open and light, this is not a day for harsh ultimatums. It is a day for *softened sovereignty* ~ choosing where your energy begins and ends with clarity, kindness, and care.

The archetype of the day is The Gentle Guardian ~ the one who protects their space with compassion, who knows their worth is not measured by availability, and who honors connection through *discernment*.

Today's symbols are graceful but firm:

— A circle drawn in sand, visible, flexible, temporary, and intentional

— Hematite, the grounding stone of boundaries, balance, and energy integrity

— The Nine of Wands, the wounded but wise one who chooses where and how to stand

— A porcupine, soft on the inside, protected with presence, not aggression

This day brings healing to those who've been taught that saying no is cruel, that self-care is selfish, or that love requires depletion.

"You are not here to disappear into everyone else," the day whispers. "You're allowed to have edges. And softness, too."

And as the soul stood in that awareness, a quiet question arrived like a breeze against the skin:

Where might I need to soften my no ~ not into a yes, but into a kind boundary I can actually live with?

Later, the soul gently revised their schedule. Declined a message. Stepped away from a conversation. Not out of withdrawal ~ but out of *respect*.

Being honest with yourself, ask:

— What do I keep saying yes to out of habit or fear?

— Where is my energy asking for protection, not punishment?

— What does a kind, loving boundary feel like ~ in action, not theory?

No big declarations. Just clear, sacred space.

Sacred Actions: Write a list of three small boundaries you'd like to try today ~ one physical, one emotional, one digital. Practice them. Notice how your body responds.

Symbolic Focus: The skin, the breath in the lower belly, the pause before saying yes.

Your Mantra for Today ~

"My boundaries are soft, clear, and sacred."

February 9 - The Day of Remembered Wholeness

A story of reclaimed truth, inner reunion, and the powerful return to the self that never truly left

There once was a soul who spent years trying to be better.

Better at feeling. Better at healing. Better at being enough.

They collected books, advice, practices ~ always reaching for the version of themselves they thought they *should* become.

But one night, under a quiet sky, the soul looked into a mirror ~ not for appearance, but for presence. And in their own reflection, they saw something they hadn't noticed in a long time:

Not improvement. Not perfection. But *recognition*.

"You're still here," they whispered. "Under it all, you never left."

And with that, something settled. Not as an achievement ~ but as a return.

February 9 carries the number 9 ~ the number of wisdom, completion, and soul integration. But this isn't about reaching a final version. It's about remembering that you were never broken to begin with.

With Aquarius still opening space for reflection and alignment, today becomes a mirror. A chance to *see yourself whole* ~ even if you're still healing, still learning, still becoming.

The archetype of the day is The Soul Rememberer ~ the one who reclaims what was never truly lost, who recognizes healing not as becoming someone new, but as *returning to who you've always been underneath the forgetting.*

The symbols of the day arrive like soft echoes:

— A mirror reflecting a steady flame

— Lapis lazuli, the stone of soul truth and ancient remembering

— The Judgement card, not about verdict, but about awakening to self

— A whale, whose song echoes across oceans of time and memory

This day brings healing for those who feel fractured by expectations, shame, or the illusion of not-enoughness. For those who've forgotten that they are not a project ~ they are a person. And a whole one, at that.

"You do not have to become someone else," the day says. "You only need to remember who you are beneath the noise."

And in that stillness, a question arises like light returning to a long-shaded room:

What part of me has always been whole ~ even when I forgot to see it?

Later, the soul sat in silence, hand over heart, and repeated softly:

"I am not a problem to solve. I am a soul to remember."

Being honest with yourself, ask:

— What versions of myself have I abandoned in the pursuit of "better"?

— What wholeness lives in me already ~ even if I don't fully believe it yet?

— What would change if I trusted that I was never broken?

They didn't feel fully healed. But they felt held. And sometimes, that's more than enough.

Sacred Actions: Choose a photograph, a memory, or a part of your body that you often criticize. Look at it gently and say:

"You are still part of me. I welcome you home."

Symbolic Focus: The solar plexus, the palms, the space behind the heart.

Your Mantra for Today ~

"I am already whole. I only needed to remember."

February 10 - The Day of Sacred Slowness

A story of patient pace, embodied time, and the quiet miracles that unfold when nothing is rushed

There once was a soul who had learned to hurry.

Hurry through healing. Hurry through conversations. Hurry through even the joyful things ~ always braced for what came next.

Stillness made them anxious. Waiting made them worry. Slowness felt like something to escape ~ not embrace.

But one day, they found themselves walking without destination. No headphones. No list. Just the rhythm of their breath and the sound of their own footsteps.

They noticed the way sunlight touched leaves. The way their muscles softened as they walked a little slower. The way *life* felt more alive when it wasn't being outrun.

"This," they thought, "is not wasted time. This is sacred time."

February 10 carries the vibration of 1 (from 1+0) ~ a number of new beginnings and intention. But today, that beginning is rooted in *slowness*. A new relationship with time. A gentle refusal to rush into becoming.

Aquarius's influence brings presence to the mind ~ but today, the soul is invited into the body. Into breath. Into *slow integration*.

The archetype of the day is The Slow Walker ~ the one who no longer rushes their transformation, who knows the deepest healing blooms *quietly*, and who meets the moment at the speed of truth.

Today's symbols are grounded, deliberate, and tender:

— A snail on a moss-covered stone, carrying home on its back

— Smoky quartz, to anchor, clear, and protect in stillness

— The Knight of Pentacles, who builds slowly, but with unwavering devotion

— A tortoise, wise and unhurried, living with presence rather than pressure

This day brings healing for those who equate speed with success. For those who were taught that urgency equals importance, or that slowing down makes you fall behind.

"You are not behind," the day whispers. "You are in rhythm with your becoming."

And in that softened moment, a powerful question emerges:

If I stopped rushing, what might I finally begin to notice, feel, or heal?

Later, the soul lit a candle ~ not to mark an occasion, but to *watch it burn*.

No multitasking. No expectation. Just presence.

Being honest with yourself, ask:

— Where in my life am I pushing too hard, too fast?

— What might be unfolding in me that needs time, not pressure?

— How can I slow down today ~ not as delay, but as devotion?

The flame flickered. The answers came… slowly. And they were enough.

Sacred Actions: Choose one thing to do half as fast today ~ eating, walking, replying. Let it be a ceremony. Let it change you.

Symbolic Focus: The legs, the back body, the pause between breaths.

Your Mantra for Today ~

"I move at the pace of my own truth. That is enough."

February 11 - The Day of Quiet Knowing

A story of deep intuition, wordless wisdom, and trusting the truth that doesn't shout

There once was a soul who craved answers.

They sought signs, chased clarity, and asked for certainty at every crossroad. They wanted proof. Direction. A voice loud enough to quiet all doubt.

But one morning, standing in stillness before a blank page, they felt something different ~ not a decision, not a fact ~ but a knowing.

It didn't explain itself. It didn't ask to be justified. It simply said:

"This is true. You already know."

The soul didn't argue. For once, they didn't second-guess. They just breathed into the quiet... and *listened*.

It wasn't logic. It wasn't fear. It was truth ~ soft and unmistakable.

February 11 carries the vibration of the master number 11 ~ intuition, illumination, and the bridge between inner and outer worlds.

On this day, your wisdom comes not from thinking, but from *feeling into what's already there.*

Aquarius adds clarity of vision, yet today, that vision turns inward. You are invited to trust what you *sense*, even if you can't yet explain it.

The archetype of the day is The Inner Oracle ~ the one who has stopped outsourcing their truth, who lets their body, their breath, and their soul speak softly into decision.

The symbols of the day are subtle, timeless, and clear:

— A closed eye glowing with inner light

— Moonstone, crystal of deep intuition and feminine insight

— The High Priestess, silent guardian of sacred inner knowing

— A white owl, perched in stillness, seeing in the dark

This day offers healing to those who doubt themselves, who've been told they're "too sensitive," or who override their inner voice in favor of external approval.

"You do not need to convince anyone," the day whispers. "You only need to *trust what you already know.*"

And in the hush that follows, a quiet question rises like mist:

What truth have I known for a long time ~ but haven't yet honored?

Later, the soul sat in silence ~ no questions, no striving. Just presence.

They placed a hand on their belly, one on their chest. And let the answers arrive as sensation, as ease, as clarity without words.

Being honest with yourself, ask:

— What decisions feel heavy... and which feel light?

— Where in my body do I feel yes? Where do I feel no?

— What would change if I stopped asking for permission ~ and started trusting my sense?

The pen moved gently. Not fast. Not forced. Just... faithfully.

Sacred Actions: Close your eyes. Place your hands over your body. Ask:

"What do I already know ~ that I've been afraid to believe?"

Trust the first feeling, even if no words come.

Symbolic Focus: The third eye, the chest center, the pulse in your fingertips.

Your Mantra for Today ~

"I trust the quiet truth that lives in me."

February 12 - The Day of Openhearted Presence

A story of vulnerability without fear, loving without agenda, and the power of simply being with what is

There once was a soul who had learned to guard their heart.

They didn't mean to become hard ~ only *safe*. They smiled in conversations, listened with care, gave what they could… but something always held back. A layer of armor. A subtle brace.

They thought they were being strong. But over time, they realized… they were lonely.

One afternoon, while sitting with someone who said nothing ~ just *sat with them* ~ the soul felt something break… quietly. Not like a wound. Like a door easing open.

It wasn't a dramatic moment. It was presence. Undemanding, unhurried, fully *there*.

"This," the soul thought, "is what my heart has been waiting for ~ not to be fixed, but to be felt."

February 12 carries the energy of 3 (from 1+2), a number of expression, connection, and creative presence. But today, the expression is not outward performance ~ it's openhearted presence.

With Aquarius offering vision and expansion, this energy asks not for more effort, but for more *availability*. To drop the roles and simply *be* ~ with another, with yourself, with the moment.

The archetype of the day is The Heart Opener ~ the one who shows up with gentle courage, who chooses love over defense, and who lets connection be *enough*.

Today's symbols radiate tenderness and truth:

— Two hands resting palm to palm, not clasping ~ just touching

— Rhodonite, for heart healing, compassion, and co-regulation

— The Three of Cups, soul-level connection and emotional support

— A horse, standing beside another, silent and steady ~ bonded through trust

This day brings healing for those who've armored their heart in the name of safety. For those who've shown up for others without ever fully letting themselves *be seen*.

"You are safe to be soft," the day whispers. "You are strong enough to be open."

And in that tenderness, a quiet question floats in:

What happens when I stop guarding my heart… and simply let it be felt?

Later, the soul practiced presence ~ not in meditation, but in *conversation*. They listened without solving. Spoke without editing. Felt without explanation.

Being honest with yourself, ask:

— What parts of me are longing to be met ~ not fixed, just seen?

— Where can I soften my presence today, and let love flow without performance?

— What would it feel like to be fully with someone ~ including myself ~ without needing to change anything?

There was no grand epiphany. Just presence. Just pulse. Just connection.

Sacred Actions: Offer your full attention ~ to someone, something, or yourself ~ for five minutes today. No distractions. Just witness, breathe, be.

Symbolic Focus: The center of the chest, the open palms, the gaze when no words are spoken.

Your Mantra for Today ~

"I meet this moment ~ and myself ~ with an open heart."

February 13 - The Day of Embodied Grace

A story of moving gently through the world, living truth through the body, and allowing every step to be a sacred offering

There once was a soul who thought grace was something earned.

They believed it came after perfection. After apology. After proving they were worthy enough to receive it.

So they tried hard ~ to be right, to be kind, to be everything they thought "graceful" meant.

But one day, while walking through a field of dry grass, the soul tripped ~ not dramatically, just enough to stumble. Enough to feel foolish.

They looked around, bracing for shame.

But the world didn't judge them. The wind still blew softly. The earth still held their feet. Their breath still moved through them.

"This," they realized, "is grace ~ not absence of imperfection, but love that stays despite it."

And for the first time, they stood not with tension, but with presence.

February 13 carries the energy of 4 (1 + 3) ~ a number of structure, steadiness, and rooted embodiment. But today, that structure doesn't confine. It *supports* you as you move through life with more softness and more sovereignty.

Under Aquarius's breathy light, the message is clear: Let your truth live through your movements, not just your mind. Let your *grace* be felt in how you walk, speak, rest, and respond ~ not to impress, but to *align*.

The archetype of the day is The Grace Carrier ~ the one who walks with humility, stands with dignity, and embodies gentleness as a form of sacred strength.

Today's symbols are quiet, grounded, and fluid:

— A curved branch bending in the breeze, never breaking

— Blue chalcedony, crystal of peace, poise, and self-acceptance

— The Strength card, but not roaring ~ smiling gently with inner trust

— A white heron, long-legged and slow-moving, every step deliberate and clear

This day brings healing for those who think grace is something given to others but not to themselves. For those who hide behind competence instead of kindness.

"You do not have to try so hard," the day whispers. "You can move with grace now ~ just as you are."

And in the stillness that follows, a quiet question stirs like silk:

What would shift if I let grace live in my body ~ not just in my ideas?

Later, the soul walked more slowly than usual. Not to delay… but to feel. They paused before reacting. They touched their own shoulder gently. They smiled ~ not to be polite, but to connect.

Being honest with yourself, ask:

— How do I move through the world when I am trying to "be enough"?

— What would graceful movement ~ thought, action, speech ~ feel like today?

— What does it mean to live with embodied self-respect, even in imperfection?

There were no gold medals for effort. Only the quiet reward of being *with themselves*, fully.

Sacred Actions: Stand still, close your eyes, and take three slow steps ~ with intention, with breath, with grace. Let your body remember:

"I am allowed to move gently."

Symbolic Focus: The spine, the knees, the rhythm of breath in walking.

Your Mantra for Today ~

"I move with grace. I live in peace with myself."

February 14 - The Day of Devoted Love

A story of steady affection, heart-deep commitment, and redefining love as something lived ~ not just felt

There once was a soul who misunderstood love.

They thought it had to be intense. That it had to sweep them off their feet. That love was supposed to feel like fire ~ constant, consuming, unmistakable.

So when love showed up as quiet presence, as someone remembering how they took their tea, or a hand resting in theirs during silence… they almost missed it.

But one day ~ this day ~ they sat alone with a memory. Not a dramatic one. Just a moment when someone stayed.

Stayed through discomfort. Stayed after the apology. Stayed when it wasn't easy or exciting ~ but *real*.

And the soul realized:

"Love isn't always lightning. Sometimes, it's choosing to show up ~ again and again ~ with care."

February 14 holds the vibration of 5 (1 + 4), the number of emotional movements, soulful change, and courageous connection. But today, that courage doesn't show off. It *stays close*. It makes love visible through *devotion* ~ the daily, grounded kind.

Under Aquarius's sky, love expands beyond romance. It becomes spacious, inclusive, unexpected. You are invited to explore love not as a performance, but as a *practice* ~ especially with yourself.

The archetype of the day is The Heart Devotee ~ the one who commits to care, not out of perfection but persistence. The one who waters love daily, not just when it blooms.

Symbols of the day pulse with quiet warmth:

— A thread tied around two fingers, worn and fraying ~ still holding

— Rose quartz, crystal of open-hearted compassion and enduring care

— The Two of Cups, not as fantasy, but as real connection and mutual presence

— A pair of elephants, leaning into each other ~ slow, strong, forever loyal

This day offers healing for those who've confused love with drama, who expect it to always feel like a rush, or who forget that devotion is often *small and sacred*.

"Love," the day whispers, "is not what you feel once. It's what you choose ~ again and again ~ in presence."

And from that still, steady space, a question unfolds like petals:

Where in my life am I being asked to love ~ not louder, but more consistently?

Later, the soul wrote a love note ~ not to a partner, but to themselves.
A soft reminder of their worth, their tenderness, their effort.

Being honest with yourself, ask:

— What does devotion mean to me ~ in love, in care, in presence?

— Who or what deserves my daily, patient affection right now ~ including parts of myself?

— How can I live love today in action, not only in emotion?

No declarations. Just devotion.

Sacred Actions: Write a love note today ~ to yourself, to someone you've taken for granted, to a dream you've nearly forgotten. Keep it simple. Keep it true.

Symbolic Focus: The chest, the back of the heart, the inner wrist pulse.

Your Mantra for Today ~

"I love with presence. I love by staying."

February 15 - The Day of Wholehearted Choice

A story of inner alignment, soulful decision, and the clarity that comes when you choose from your center ~ not your fear

There once was a soul who lived in the waiting room of their own life.

Always hesitating. Always wondering. Always half-in, half-out of every decision ~ afraid to choose wrong, afraid to choose too soon, afraid to choose at all.

They became masters of maybe. Carried a thousand options like weight on their back.

But one day ~ quiet and clear ~ the soul stood at a crossroads, and for once, instead of listing pros and cons, they listened to their body.

Their breath slowed.

Their stomach softened.

Their heart said, not in words but in knowing:

"This way. Not because it's perfect. But because it's *true* for you."

And they chose. Not to please. Not to prove. But to *live in alignment with themselves.*

February 15 carries the number 6 (1 + 5), a number of balance, values, and heart-centered discernment. Today invites you to remember: choice is not pressure ~ it is power. And that power lives in your *wholeness.*

With Aquarius still offering vision and fresh perspective, today is not about impulsive action. It's about *clear-hearted commitment* ~ not just choosing, but *standing fully behind what you choose.*

The archetype of the day is The Soul Chooser ~ the one who no longer fragments themselves across every possibility, but brings all of who they are into every decision they make.

Today's symbols are steady, grounded, and brave:

— A single arrow released from a calm hand

— Tiger's eye, the stone of clear intention and grounded courage

— The Two of Wands, standing with vision, choosing from power ~ not panic

— A mountain goat, choosing each step with care, but never doubting the climb

This day offers healing for those who struggle with self-trust. For those who second-guess their choices before, during, and after. For those who delay out of fear they'll lose something ~ forgetting that *wholeness can never be lost by choosing yourself.*

"You are allowed to choose," the day whispers. "Not from fear. From fullness."

And in that breath, a bold and tender question arises:

What would I choose today if I trusted that my wholeness would hold me ~ no matter the outcome?

Later, the soul looked at a decision they'd been circling for weeks. They placed a hand on their heart and said:

"I choose this. With all of me. Not because it's easy ~ but because it's mine."

Being honest with yourself, ask:

— What am I avoiding choosing ~ and what deeper truth is underneath that avoidance?

— What decision would bring me closer to my truth, even if it feels risky?

— What part of me do I need to bring home before I can choose from wholeness?

Sacred Actions: Choose one thing today ~ small or large ~ and choose it fully. Speak it aloud. Stand behind it. Let your body feel the difference between "maybe" and "yes."

Symbolic Focus: The solar plexus, the spine, the breath just before commitment.

Your Mantra for Today ~

"I choose from my center. My truth leads me forward."

February 16 - The Day of Soul Restoration

A story of deep replenishment, sacred stillness, and the healing that comes not from doing more, but from coming home to yourself

There once was a soul who didn't know how tired they were.

They were functioning. Smiling. Helping. Showing up. But underneath it all was an ache ~ not just in the body, but in the *being*.

They thought they needed a vacation. They thought they needed sleep. But what they truly needed… was to return to themselves.

One morning, instead of powering through, they paused.

They turned off the noise. Put down the phone. Closed their eyes ~ not to escape, but to listen inwardly.

And in that pause, they felt it:

"I miss me."

Not the productive version. Not the polished one. The soft, breathing, present self that had been waiting patiently beneath all the effort.

And so, they whispered back:

"I'm here now. I'm ready to return."

February 16 carries the number 7 (1 + 6), a number of spiritual depth, inner truth, and healing through reflection. Today is a day not for striving ~ but for *restoring*.

With Aquarius still present in the skies, the message becomes clear:
You cannot serve the world from depletion. You cannot meet others if you've left yourself.

The archetype of the day is The Inner Healer ~ the one who knows that restoration is not indulgence ~ it is necessity. The one who honors healing not as a destination, but as a rhythm.

Symbols for today invite you inward, gently:

— A cup being filled slowly from a mountain spring

— Lepidolite, a crystal of nervous system calm and emotional reset

— The Four of Swords, a sacred pause for soul recovery

— A deer, lying in tall grass, breathing deeply, sensing safety

This day brings healing for those who've carried more than their share. For those who've given until empty. For those who've confused restoration with laziness.

"You do not need to be exhausted to be worthy," the day whispers.

"You are allowed to come home to yourself."

And in that permission, a gentle question emerges:

What would it mean to give myself back to me today ~ piece by piece, breath by breath?

Later, the soul did something uncharacteristically kind. They stopped mid-task. Laid down. Or took a walk. Or lit a candle without needing a reason.

Being honest with yourself, ask:

— What part of me has been stretched thin ~ and what

  does it need to soften?

— Where have I ignored the call to rest because I felt I

  didn't deserve it?

— What does restoration look like for me today ~

  physically, emotionally, spiritually?

They didn't need to solve everything. They only needed to *restore the connection to their own essence.*

Sacred Actions: Cancel one non-essential task today. Replace it with something that restores you ~ even for 10 minutes. Say:

"This is for me. And that matters."

Symbolic Focus: The lower back, the breath in the ribs, the moment between effort and ease.

Your Mantra for Today ~

"I return to myself. My restoration is sacred."

February 17 - The Day of Inner Permission

A story of quiet liberation, unspoken rules, and the deep healing that begins when you allow yourself to be fully, truly you

There once was a soul who waited for permission.

To rest. To speak. To shine. To stop trying so hard.

They waited for someone to say, *"It's okay now. You can let go. You can just be."*

But no one ever said it.

Until one day ~ quiet and tender ~ the soul realized they were the only one who could offer what they'd always craved.

They stood in front of a mirror, looked into their own tired eyes, and said:

"You don't need a reason. You need *permission*. And I give it to you now."

In that moment, the chains weren't broken. They were simply set down ~ gently, by choice.

February 17 carries the number 8 (1 + 7), a number of strength, autonomy, and personal power. But this day's power isn't loud. It's not about control ~ it's about inner authority.

Aquarius still offers its clarifying wind, clearing out outdated scripts. The invitation is this: What rules have you been following that no longer serve who you are now? And what might shift if you said to yourself: *"You are allowed."*

The archetype of the day is The Permission Giver ~ the one who reclaims their own authority, who no longer waits for external validation, and who grants themselves space to breathe, change, speak, soften, rest, begin.

Today's symbols feel like keys ~ gentle and firm:

— An open door with light streaming through

— Sunstone, crystal of empowerment, joy, and permission to thrive

— The Eight of Swords, reversed ~ the moment you realize the cage was never locked

This day offers healing for those who were taught they had to earn space, prove worth, or wait for approval. For those whose brilliance has been dimmed by self-policing and outdated permission slips.

"You are allowed," the day says, "to choose for yourself ~ fully, freely, now."

And in the quiet after, a bold question rises like sunlight over a locked gate:

What am I waiting for permission to do, feel, become ~ that I can grant myself today?

Later, the soul wrote a permission slip on a napkin, a notebook, or the palm of their hand. It said:

"I allow myself to rest." "I allow myself to not explain." "I allow myself to want what I want."

Being honest with yourself, ask:

— What would I choose if I didn't need anyone to agree with me?

— What permission have I been denying myself ~ that I now choose to give freely?

— How does it feel to let myself be fully human, without apology?

They felt no guilt. Only *space.*

Sacred Actions: Write your own permission slip today. Use the words:

"I allow myself to…"

Then follow through. No justification. Just truth.

Symbolic Focus: The throat, the solar plexus, the back of the shoulders.

Your Mantra for Today ~

"I no longer wait. I give myself permission."

February 18 - The Day of Deep Integration

A story of weaving the pieces, holding the contradictions, and becoming whole without needing to be finished

There once was a soul who believed healing had a finish line.

That one day, they would feel clear. Certain. Simple. That all the parts would click into place and make perfect sense.

So they worked hard ~ unpacked their past, rewrote their patterns, learned every insight they could find.

But something still felt... complex.

Then one afternoon, while organizing old journals, the soul noticed something strange: Every version of themselves still lived in those pages ~ the brave one, the scared one, the angry one, the awakening one.

And for the first time, they didn't cringe. They didn't disown.

They felt a thread running through it all. Not a straight line. A spiral. A weaving.

"I am not a contradiction," they whispered. "I am a convergence."

February 18 carries the energy of 9 (1 + 8), the number of completion, integration, and soul wisdom. But this isn't a "done" energy ~ it's an invitation to bring all parts of yourself *into belonging.*

In the final day of Aquarius season, before the shift into Pisces, this moment becomes a spiritual bridge ~ from thought to feeling, from separation to wholeness.

The archetype of the day is The Soul Weaver ~ the one who doesn't throw out old selves, but braids them into being. The one who knows that your healing doesn't erase your story ~ it *includes it all.*

Today's symbols hum with layered harmony:

— A braided cord, strong not despite difference, but because of it

— Labradorite, crystal of multidimensional truth and integration

— The Temperance card, mixing what once felt separate into a sacred whole

— A spider, patiently spinning its web ~ one strand, one memory, one truth at a time

This day brings healing for those who feel fragmented. For those who think they have to "figure it all out" before they can be at peace. For those who fear that past versions of themselves disqualify them from present joy.

"You are not broken," the day says. "You are becoming *woven*."

And in that realization, a deep question echoes inward:

What parts of me have I left behind… that now want to be brought back home?

Later, the soul took a deep breath. Not to calm down ~ but to *arrive*. They touched their chest and said,

"All of me belongs here."

Being honest with yourself, ask:

— What stories or selves have I outgrown ~ but still carry shame around?

— What would integration look like if it didn't mean solving… just embracing?

— How might I hold complexity today ~ without trying to simplify who I am?

The answers weren't tidy. But they felt *true*.

Sacred Actions: Choose one past version of yourself to honor today ~ through a letter, a small ritual, or a whispered thank you. Let them know: *"You're part of the whole."*

A spiral woven from threads of many colors, converging toward the center ~ a sacred tapestry of self.

Symbolic Focus: The heart, the navel, the spine.

Your Mantra for Today ~

"I am the sum of every part. I weave them into wholeness."

February 19 - The Day of Soul Surrender

A story of letting go, trusting the tides, and finding peace not through control ~ but through deep, sacred release

There once was a soul who tried to hold it all together.

The plans. The feelings. The roles. The outcomes. They clutched every piece of life like it was their responsibility to shape it, fix it, carry it all.

Control felt like safety. Surrender felt like danger. Until the weight became too much ~ and holding on began to hurt more than letting go.

One evening, they stood by a body of water ~ still, infinite.

They placed their palms downward. Exhaled. And whispered not in defeat, but in trust:

"I release. I allow. I trust the flow."

The water didn't change. But something inside them did.

They didn't disappear. They softened.

They didn't drown. They *floated*.

February 19 marks the beginning of Pisces season and carries the number 1 (1 + 9 = 10 → 1), a number of new beginnings. But this "beginning" doesn't start with action. It begins with surrender ~ a return to flow, mystery, and faith in something larger than logic.

The Piscean waters call you into trust without a map. This is the soul's baptism ~ a cleansing, a softening, a remembering that you are not meant to control the current ~ only to *move with it*.

The archetype of the day is The Surrendered One ~ not passive, but open. Not powerless, but aligned. The one who knows that surrender isn't giving up ~ it's giving *into*.

Today's symbols are deep, fluid, and reverent:

— A leaf floating downstream, carried without resistance

— Aquamarine, crystal of emotional release and intuitive flow

— The Hanged Man, offering perspective through stillness and surrender

— A whale, massive and gentle, carried by ocean currents deeper than thought

This day brings healing for those who cling out of fear ~ who've built lives on control, perfectionism, or endless "doing." For those who long to let go, but don't know how.

"You don't need to have all the answers," the day says. "You only need to trust the current you're already in."

And in that moment, a soft, brave question rises like a tide:

What would I feel if I stopped gripping and started allowing?

Later, the soul placed one hand on their heart, one on their belly, and breathed slowly.

They didn't fix anything. They didn't plan. They *allowed*.

Being honest with yourself, ask:

— What am I still holding that is ready to be released?

— Where might surrender be safer than I've been taught to believe?

— How does my body feel when I stop trying to control what comes next?

They didn't seek outcomes. They opened to *experience*.

Sacred Actions: Let something be unfinished today. Let something unfold without your interference. Whisper:

"I trust the unfolding. I release the need to manage what is already becoming."

Symbolic Focus: The palms, the breath in the hips, the space behind the heart.

Your Mantra for Today ~

"I surrender what I cannot carry. I trust what I cannot see."

February 20 - The Day of Compassion and Flow

A story of empathy without overwhelm, softness without sacrifice, and learning to let love move through you ~ not drain you

There once was a soul who felt everything.

They could sense tension in a room before words were spoken. They carried others' pain as if it were their own. Their empathy was vast ~ but so was their exhaustion.

They thought compassion meant absorbing it all. That to be kind, they had to give endlessly. That to help, they had to hurt.

But one day, standing near a stream, they watched the water curve gently around stones ~ not crashing, not stopping, *flowing*.

And they realized:

"Compassion doesn't mean losing myself in others. It means staying with myself *as I love them*."

They didn't stop feeling deeply. They just stopped emptying themselves to do it.

February 20 carries the energy of 2 (2 + 0) ~ a number of connection, intuition, and emotional resonance. In Pisces season, this number takes on the texture of *feeling everything* ~ but today offers a new way to relate to that sensitivity: through compassionate boundaries and flow.

The archetype of the day is The Compassionate Channel ~ the one who lets love move *through* them, not *into* them like a flood. The one who tends their own shore while still meeting others at the water's edge.

Today's symbols are fluid, steady, and wise:

— A stream flowing between two banks, moving without flooding

— Chrysoprase, a crystal for compassion, forgiveness, and heart-centered grace

— The Queen of Cups, emotionally attuned, yet anchored in her own vessel

— A jellyfish, drifting with current ~ soft, but with inner structure

This day offers healing for the empaths, the feelers, the nurturers. For those who equate love with sacrifice, or kindness with overextension.

"You can be soft," the day whispers, "without disappearing. You can feel… and still *flow*."

And in that soft realization, a life-giving question emerges:

What does it look like to feel deeply ~ without losing myself in the process?

Later, the soul sat beside a plant, a candle, or a window ~ something alive, something gentle. They placed a hand over their heart and whispered:

"It is safe to feel. It is safe to flow. It is safe to stay with myself."

Being honest with yourself, ask:

— Where have I confused compassion with self-abandonment?

— How can I be present with others while staying rooted in myself?

— What are my signs that I'm flowing… versus being drained?

Their words became a stream ~ not rushed, not blocked ~ just honest, and *alive*.

Sacred Actions: Offer compassion today. Offer it without overextending. Choose one person or moment to meet *with care and boundary.* Say silently:

"I am here with you, and I am still with me."

Symbolic Focus: The heart, the solar plexus, the boundary between skin and air.

Your Mantra for Today ~

"My compassion flows. My self remains."

February 21 - The Day of Trustful Softness

A story of releasing defensiveness, leaning into gentleness, and discovering that true safety lives in being fully open

There once was a soul who mistook softness for weakness.

They learned to brace. To analyze before feeling. To meet the world with a quiet shield ~ not out of anger, but out of history.

They had once been hurt while they were soft. So they became strong ~ but in that strength, they became *hard*.

Then one day, they held a flower ~ a bloom so delicate it seemed impossible that it had survived wind, rain, frost. And yet, there it was.

Unfolded. Alive.

"Softness," the soul realized, "isn't what breaks. It's what bends and *still chooses to open again*."

And in that breath, the armor didn't crack ~ it *melted*.

February 21 holds the energy of 3 (2 + 1), the number of expression, vulnerability, and open-hearted communication. In Pisces' gentle waters, today invites you to live from your tenderness ~ not as a flaw, but as a deep form of trust.

This is not performative vulnerability. This is softness that comes from strength. This is emotional openness that says: *"I know how to close ~ and I choose not to today."*

The archetype of the day is The Courageous Bloom ~ the one who dares to stay open even after storms, who knows that true resilience is not resistance ~ it's trust in your *own unfolding*.

Today's symbols shimmer with subtle power:

— A flower opening in early spring, despite the cold air

— Morganite, crystal of heart expansion, healing, and emotional bravery

— The Star card, a return to faith, hope, and sacred vulnerability

— A baby animal, small but sure ~ no pretense, only presence

This day brings healing for those who have hidden behind strength, who were told to toughen up, who became sharp so they wouldn't be seen as soft.

"You are allowed to be gentle," the day whispers. "You are safe enough to be real."

And in that moment, a sacred question unfolds like a petal:

What part of me is ready to soften ~ not because it's easy, but because it's time?

Later, the soul let their face relax. Spoke slower. Touched their own arm like they would a child's ~ with care, not critique.

Being honest with yourself, ask:

— Where have I armored myself against softness?

— What would it feel like to let my tenderness be visible ~ even in small ways?

— What does "emotional safety" look like when it comes from inside me, not from outside validation?

No fixing. No rushing. Just soft return.

Sacred Actions: Let one interaction today be softer than usual ~ whether with yourself or another. Speak gently. Pause often. Allow vulnerability to lead the moment.

Symbolic Focus: The throat, the heart, the corners of the eyes.

Your Mantra for Today ~

"My softness is not a risk ~ it is a return to trust."

February 22 - The Day of Sacred Alignment

A story of inner balance, soulful order, and remembering that when all parts of you align ~ even for a moment ~ life begins to flow

There once was a soul who lived in pieces.

They were thoughtful, but not grounded. Creative, but unstructured. Spiritual, but disconnected from the body. Each part of them was alive ~ but *nothing worked together*.

They moved through life like a beautiful, scattered constellation ~ never quite whole, always a little out of sync.

Until one day, they sat down, placed both feet on the ground, closed their eyes, and simply asked:

"What would it feel like if all of me moved in the same direction?"

For the first time, they felt it ~ their mind, body, heart, and spirit... *clicking into place.* Not perfectly. Not forever.

But enough.

Enough to feel the pulse of alignment. Enough to remember what it means to be fully *themselves.*

February 22 carries the powerful master number 22 ~ the number of sacred structure, vision rooted in reality, and energetic coherence. In the intuitive waters of Pisces, this becomes more than planning ~ it becomes embodied alignment.

This day calls for integration: Thoughts that serve feelings. Actions that serve intentions. Spirituality that lives in your *real life.*

The archetype of the day is The Aligned Architect ~ the one who builds their inner world with reverence, who organizes not out of control, but out of devotion to wholeness.

Today's symbols move with calm power:

— A circle inside a square, balanced yet spacious

— Fluorite, for mental clarity, energetic alignment, and focus

— The Justice card, not about punishment ~ about harmony and truth

— A crane, standing tall and still, wings tucked, perfectly centered

This day offers healing for those who feel pulled in too many directions ~ who've been spiritual but ungrounded, emotional but scattered, insightful but disembodied.

"You don't need to do more," the day says. "You need to align what you already are."

And in that deep pause, a resonant question rises:

What part of me is out of sync ~ and what wants to return to center?

Later, the soul lit a candle and did *one thing* with their whole self. Not multitasking. Not rushing. Just… integrity.

Being honest with yourself, ask:

— Where am I living out of alignment ~ doing what I don't believe, saying what I don't feel?

— What might shift if my body, heart, mind, and spirit worked together ~ not apart?

— What's one step I can take today that honors my full self, not just one part of me?

They didn't chase balance. They *became* it.

Sacred Actions: Choose a part of your life ~ a habit, a relationship, a routine ~ and ask:

"Does this align with who I really am?"

Adjust one small thing today so that your answer can be yes.

Symbolic Focus: The hips, the feet, the crown of the head.

Your Mantra for Today ~

"When all of me aligns, I move with truth."

February 23 - The Day of Rooted Sensitivity

A story of feeling deeply without floating away, anchoring empathy in strength, and discovering that sensitivity is a superpower when grounded in truth

There once was a soul who felt everything ~ but had nowhere to land.

They picked up the moods of others. They sensed pain in silence. They wept at beauty… and at chaos.

But they often felt untethered. Like a kite with a cut string ~ moved by every wind, never sure what was *theirs* and what belonged to someone else.

Then one morning, they stood barefoot in the grass. No shoes. No noise. No shield. They felt the earth beneath them ~ solid, steady, alive.

"Feel it all," the earth whispered. "But feel it from *here*."

The soul didn't stop being sensitive. They simply stopped being swept away by it.

And in that moment, their emotions became roots instead of waves.

February 23 carries the energy of 7 (2 + 3), a number of spiritual reflection, emotional depth, and the sacred pause. But today, that depth is not about escaping the world ~ it's about learning how to be fully in it, while staying *centered.*

With Pisces still flowing through the air, you're invited to keep your heart wide open ~ but also held.

The archetype of the day is The Grounded Empath ~ the one who loves without leaking, who listens without losing themselves, and who knows that deep sensitivity *requires deep anchoring.*

Today's symbols offer soft strength:

— A tree swaying in wind, its roots deep in soil

— Black tourmaline, crystal of energetic boundaries and grounded presence

— The King of Cups, emotionally mature, calm amid chaos

— An otter, playful, intuitive, but always returning to its den

This day brings healing for those who feel "too much" ~ too emotional, too reactive, too tender. It reminds you:

"Your feelings are not flaws. They are *signals.* And you get to feel them *safely.*"

And from that rooted calm, a clarifying question arises:

How can I honor my emotional depth ~ while also staying anchored in what's real for me?

Later, the soul placed a hand on their chest, one on their lower belly, and breathed slowly.

They didn't suppress.

They didn't spiral.

They *stayed.*

Being honest with yourself, ask:

— What emotions of mine do I tend to run from ~ and why?

— What's the difference between being flooded... and being present?

— How can I support my nervous system today so it feels safe to feel?

The truth wasn't overwhelming. It was *embodied.*

Sacred Actions: Walk barefoot on grass, earth, tile ~ whatever is solid. As you walk, say silently:

"I feel deeply, and I stay with myself."

Symbolic Focus: The feet, the hips, the base of the spine.

Your Mantra for Today ~

"I am grounded in my sensitivity. I feel without floating away."

February 24 - The Day of Embodied Presence

A story of returning to the body, honoring the now, and learning that being fully here is the most sacred place you can be

There once was a soul who lived mostly in their mind.

They planned, analyzed, remembered, dreamed. They could map every possibility ~ except the one unfolding in *this very moment*.

The present felt slippery. The body, unfamiliar. They were often everywhere but here.

But one afternoon, they sat with their feet on the ground and their hand resting over their heart ~ not trying to meditate, not trying to escape. Just... *being*.

They noticed a breath. Then another. Then the soft rhythm of their heart ~ not asking for anything. Just *being alive*.

And in that small stillness, they heard the quiet truth:

"You don't need to go anywhere to arrive. You're already here."

February 24 carries the energy of 8 (2 + 4), the number of embodied power, integration, and grounded presence. Today reminds you that you don't need to transcend your life ~ you need to *inhabit* it.

In Pisces season, where it's easy to drift or dissociate, this day invites a sacred *return* ~ not to a task, a goal, or a role… but to your *own skin*.

The archetype of the day is The Present Vessel ~ the one who realizes that the body is not a barrier to spirituality, but a bridge. That presence isn't something to strive for ~ it's something to *land in*.

Today's symbols offer gentle anchors:

— A smooth river stone, heavy in the palm, cool and real

— Carnelian, crystal of life force, vitality, and grounded passion

— The Ace of Pentacles, the seed of presence, planted in the now

— A tortoise, slow and steady, always home in its shell

This day brings healing for those who live in their heads, dissociate from their body, or struggle to stay with the moment. For those who feel too much, too fast ~ and need to remember that *now* is where the truth lives.

"Come back," the day says. "Not to the past. Not to the future. But to your own breath."

And in that pause, a simple, powerful question arises:

What part of me is asking to be felt ~ right now, right here, without judgment?

Later, the soul touched their arms with care. Ran fingers through their hair. Took a walk without headphones, felt their feet meet the earth. Not to perform presence ~ to *be it.*

Being honest with yourself, ask:

— What sensations am I aware of right now? What's happening in my body beneath thought?

— Where do I leave the moment ~ and what would help me stay?

— How can I honor my body today as the sacred place where my soul lives?

They didn't try to transcend. They *arrived.*

Sacred Actions: Place one hand on your body today ~ belly, chest, thigh, wherever feels grounding ~ and say aloud:

"I am here. I am home in me."

Feel it land.

Symbolic Focus: The soles of the feet, the lower spine, the skin's surface.

Your Mantra for Today ~

"I return to this moment. My body is where I begin."

February 25 - The Day of Soul Silence

A story of sacred quiet, inner attunement, and remembering that some truths only reveal themselves when everything else falls away

There once was a soul surrounded by sound.

Chatter, updates, expectations, information ~ the endless hum of the world. They had grown so used to the noise, they forgot what silence even felt like.

But one morning, long before the world had woken, they stepped outside. No phone. No shoes. Just air and sky.

The stillness was so complete, it startled them.

No answers. No commentary. Just the subtle rhythm of breath, heartbeat, birdcall, breeze.

And then… something within them stirred. A knowing not spoken, but sensed.

"This," the soul thought, "is where I hear what matters."

In that silence, their soul didn't speak loudly. It simply became *clear.*

February 25 carries the number 9 (2 + 5), the number of completion, integration, and inward mastery. During Pisces season, this day becomes a sanctuary ~ a sacred threshold where words fall away, and truth *arrives*.

Today is not for performing, planning, or perfecting. It's for listening beyond sound. For meeting yourself not in thought, but in stillness.

The archetype of the day is The Inner Listener ~ the one who waits patiently in the hush, who honors what arises only in silence, and who knows that soul language is quiet, but *unmistakable*.

Today's symbols are soft, spacious, and echoing:

— A single white feather drifting in still air

— Scolecite, a crystal of deep peace, dreamwork, and soul-level attunement

— The Four of Swords, not a retreat ~ a recalibration

— A snowy owl, silent in flight, holding wisdom that waits to be invited

This day brings healing for those who fear silence, who fill their days with noise to escape their own depths, or who confuse stillness with stagnation.

"You are not alone in the silence," the day whispers. "You are *meeting yourself* there."

And in that sacred stillness, a gentle question arises:

What truth has been trying to reach me ~ that I've been too loud to hear?

Later, the soul did nothing for five whole minutes.

Not meditation. Not thinking. Just breathing.

Letting the silence surround them like a soft blanket of truth. Being honest with yourself, ask:

— When was the last time I truly let myself be still?

— What feelings or insights are waiting in the quiet parts of me?

— What does my soul sound like when the world goes quiet?

The answers came slowly. But they came from *within*.

Sacred Actions: Take a silence walk or sit today ~ no media, no music, no words. Just presence. Whisper before you begin:

"I am here. I am listening."

Symbolic Focus: The ears, the chest, the breath in the pause between inhale and exhale.

Your Mantra for Today ~

"In silence, my soul speaks."

February 26 - The Day of Inner Sovereignty

A story of quiet authority, self-leadership, and the moment you realize you no longer need to be chosen ~ because you've chosen yourself

There once was a soul who spent years seeking direction.

They asked for signs. Waited for approval. Bent themselves into shapes to fit expectations. They looked outward for the crown ~ the invitation to finally feel whole.

But one day, after a long period of reflection, they stood in front of a mirror ~ tired, honest, ready.

And something shifted.

Not because someone gave them permission. Not because the path became clear. But because they whispered,

"I choose me. Not later. Now."

And in that moment, they didn't rise with arrogance. They stood with quiet *authority* ~ the kind that comes not from others… but from deep alignment within.

February 26 holds the energy of 1 (2 + 6 = 8 → 8 + 1 = 9 → 9 + 1 = 10 → 1), the number of beginnings ~ this time born from completion. This is *not* the start of something impulsive. It is the embodiment of sovereignty ~ the realization that your life is yours to walk.

Pisces season adds soulful depth, asking you to lead not from ego, but from essence.

The archetype of the day is The Inner Monarch ~ the one who rules their own life from the inside out.

Not to control. Not to impress. But to live in truth without apology.

Today's symbols carry sacred power, grounded and noble:

— A golden crown resting on moss, humble and earned

— Garnet, a crystal of life force, grounding, and empowered embodiment

— The Emperor card, sacred structure guided by wisdom, not dominance

— A lioness, steady in her stride, protective, soft, self-directed

This day brings healing for those who defer too often, who have waited too long to choose themselves, or who believe that self-leadership must mean separation from others.

"You are not a guest in your own life," the day whispers. "You are the one who gets to say yes. Or no. Or begin."

And in that bold breath, a question forms like a vow:

What would I do today if I led myself with truth, not hesitation?

Later, the soul stood tall ~ not to be seen, but to feel their own presence.

They didn't take over the room.

They simply took *their place* in it.

Being honest with yourself, ask:

— Where am I still waiting for someone else to choose or validate me?

— What does self-leadership look like when guided by heart, not ego?

— What choice have I delayed out of fear that I'm not "enough" to make it?

The answers were sovereign. Because they were finally *self-given*.

Sacred Actions: Declare one boundary, choice, or vision aloud today. Say it to yourself. Write it. Walk it. Whisper:

"I lead myself from within."

Symbolic Focus: The spine, the solar plexus, the space behind the voice.

Your Mantra for Today ~

"I am the authority in my life. I choose me."

February 27 - The Day of Soul and Belonging

A story of coming home to yourself, finding connection without performance, and remembering that you were never meant to fit ~ you were meant to belong

There once was a soul who tried to earn belonging.

They changed their voice to match the room. Dimmed their light to avoid standing out. Tried on identities like clothing ~ hoping one would finally feel like *home*.

And though they were accepted… they never felt *seen*.

But one quiet evening, sitting alone with no one to impress, they asked:

"What would it feel like to belong without having to perform?"

The answer didn't come in words. It came in stillness.

In breath that didn't shrink. In a spine that didn't hunch. In a self that didn't flinch under its own gaze.

"This," the soul whispered, "is what it feels like to belong ~ to *me*."

February 27 carries the energy of 2 + 7 = 9, the number of deep wisdom, inner truth, and soulful return. In the wide waters of Pisces, today invites you not into a group ~ but into *yourself*. Not into fitting in ~ but into *belonging as you are*.

The archetype of the day is The Homecoming Soul ~ the one who stops asking where they fit and starts asking where they *feel free*. The one who creates space for others to be whole by first *being whole themselves*.

Today's symbols offer warmth, presence, and real connection:

— A campfire surrounded by open seats, no performance required

— Rhodochrosite, crystal of self-compassion and heartful belonging

— The Ten of Cups, not perfection ~ but authentic, resonant connection

— A wolf, howling alone and together, loyal to their own path and pack

This day brings healing for those who've masked to be accepted, who've questioned their worth in every room, or who've longed for connection but lost themselves trying to get it.

"You don't belong because of who you pretend to be," the day whispers. "You belong because of who you *already are*."

And from that truth, a tender question blooms like a welcome:

Where do I feel most like myself ~ and how can I build more of that into my life?

Later, the soul stood in front of the mirror and said not "I should," not "I'll be better," but simply:

"I am already worthy of belonging ~ as I am."

Being honest with yourself, ask:

— What relationships or spaces allow me to show up fully ~ unfiltered?

— What parts of myself have I hidden in exchange for approval?

— What does it mean to belong to myself ~ and how can I honor that today?

No more fitting in. Just *falling into place* ~ inside.

Sacred Actions: Reach out to someone who sees you as you are ~ or spend 10 minutes doing something that reconnects you with your authentic self. Say silently:

"I belong. Especially when I'm real."

Symbolic Focus: The back of the heart, the base of the throat, the soles of the feet touching ground.

Your Mantra for Today ~

"I do not fit in. I belong ~ to myself, to this life, to what's real."

February 28 - The Day of Sacred Closure

A story of endings with grace, cycles honored not avoided, and the quiet empowerment that comes when you choose to release with love

There once was a soul who feared endings.

They held on too long. To relationships. To dreams. To old stories. Not because they didn't know it was time ~ but because letting go felt like failure.

Until one day, standing under a dusky sky at the edge of a season's end, they noticed the trees.

How they shed. How they trusted. How they let go ~ not in grief, but in rhythm.

"Endings," the soul realized, "are not breaks in the story. They *are* the story."

And just like that, they stopped clinging. Not because they stopped caring ~ but because they started *trusting*.

February 28 carries the vibration of 1 (2 + 8 = 10 → 1), the number of new beginnings. But today, it arises from something deeper: an ending made whole. In the soft currents of Pisces, this is not a door slamming shut ~ it's a candle quietly going out, leaving warmth in its place.

The archetype of the day is The Graceful Releaser ~ the one who walks to the edge with reverence, who closes the chapter with love, and who knows that letting go is not weakness ~ it's *wisdom*.

Today's symbols embody reflection, completion, and freedom:

— A book with its final page turned, gently closed by hand

— Smoky quartz, crystal of release, grounding, and spiritual transition

— The Death card, misunderstood ~ not an ending, but a transformation

— A phoenix feather, left behind in ash, glowing at the tip

This day brings healing for those who fear loss, who hold on past the moment, or who avoid goodbyes because they don't yet trust what comes next.

"Not all things are meant to last forever," the day whispers. "But all things are meant to leave you changed."

And in that quiet knowing, a question forms like a soft exhale:

What am I being asked to close today ~ not out of bitterness, but as an act of love?

Later, the soul wrote a letter. Maybe to someone. Maybe to a dream. Maybe to a part of themselves.

They didn't send it. They didn't have to. It was the writing that set them free.

Being honest with yourself, ask:

— What chapter of my life is gently asking to close ~ and am I listening?

— What emotions do I avoid by refusing to end what's already complete?

— What might open when I create closure not with anger, but with grace?

They folded the page. And in doing so, turned one inside themselves.

Sacred Actions: Mark something complete today ~ a pattern, a plan, a relationship, a version of yourself. Light a candle or speak it aloud. Say:

"Thank you. I release you. I am free."

Symbolic Focus: The hands releasing, the breath on the exhale, the space between the eyebrows.

Your Mantra for Today ~

"I honor what ends. I trust what comes."

February 29 - The Day of Timeless Wonder

A story of rare portals, divine pauses, and the magic that happens when time makes space for mystery

There once was a soul who lived by the calendar.

They counted days, set deadlines, tracked progress. Their life was measured ~ forward motion, consistent pace, always accounted for.

But once every four years, something unusual happened. A day appeared that wasn't *supposed* to be there. A bonus. A glitch. A cosmic wink.

February 29. The soul paused.

"What if," they thought, "this day isn't just extra... it's *enchanted?*"

Not in the loud way. Not in fireworks. But in the space it offered ~ a day between the lines, outside the rules of regular time.

And in that rare opening, the soul stopped counting. They *wondered*.

February 29 holds the energy of 11 (2 + 9 = 11), a master number of intuition, insight, and spiritual portals. And because it only appears once every four years, its message is clear:

This is not just a day. It is a *threshold*.

Pisces deepens the magic, reminding you that not all time is linear ~ and not all growth is measurable. Leap Day invites you to step out of routine and into reverence for the unplanned, the uncommon, the unknown.

The archetype of the day is The Time Weaver ~ the one who understands that time is not fixed, that soul expansion happens in pauses, and that miracles often arrive *between the expected moments*.

Today's symbols shimmer with rare magic:

— A clock with no hands, glowing in moonlight

— Moonstone or labradorite, for liminal space, intuitive vision, and wonder

— The Wheel of Fortune, turning not at random, but at divine intervals

— A leaping deer, mid-air ~ graceful, suspended, belonging to neither ground nor sky

This day brings healing for those caught in cycles, overwhelmed by structure, or afraid of the unknown. For those who need space, surprise, or an energetic reset.

"You are outside of ordinary time today," the day whispers. "Anything is possible ~ not because you control it, but because you don't."

And from that wondrous pause, a question spirals through your soul:

If I stopped measuring today… what magic might find me?

Later, the soul lit a candle not for action, but for invitation. They asked no questions. They made no plans. They simply said:

"I am open. Surprise me."

Being honest with yourself, ask:

— What have I been trying to force that might need mystery instead?

— What wants to unfold in my life without being scheduled or solved?

— How might I live today ~ this rare day ~ as a ceremony of wonder?

No answers. Just awe.

Sacred Actions: Do something today you wouldn't normally do. Say yes to what surprises you. Treat the day like a pocket of magic and ask yourself:

"If this day is a gift, how will I honor it?"

Symbolic Focus: The third eye, the soles of the feet, the breath when you laugh unexpectedly.

Your Mantra for Today ~

"I live today outside of time. I open to wonder."

February Reflection

The Soft Opening: Honoring Vulnerability, Growth, and Grace

February was not a grand unfurling. It was a quiet loosening. The frost began to lift ~ not all at once, but enough to feel what lives beneath it.

You've spent this month noticing the *origins* of your inner opening ~ the small shifts, the raw edges, the ways your soul began to stretch toward warmth again.

This was not about confidence. It was about *courage*. Not about visibility ~ but *emotional truth*. Before you step into March, pause and reflect:

What Has Opened in Me?

Let your answers be felt, not forced.

- What emotional layer began to loosen this month ~ and what did it reveal?
- Where did I choose softness when I could have chosen armor?
- Which moment surprised me with its tenderness, honesty, or truth?
- What relationship ~ with myself or another ~ began to shift toward healing?
- Where did I take a risk by being seen, even just a little more fully?

Emerging Themes to Carry Forward

Growth doesn't announce itself with noise. It often arrives in *vulnerable whispers*.

This month, perhaps you discovered:

- That softness is not weakness
- That tears can be a form of release, not breakdown
- That real connection requires real presence
- That you are allowed to unfold slowly ~ and safely

Even the tiniest opening is proof that the soul is ready.

Integration Practice

Create a "moment jar."

Write down one word or phrase from February that represents something meaningful you learned, felt, or became.

Fold it. Place it in a small jar, bowl, or envelope. Keep this practice going month by month. Let it become your personal archive of becoming.

Then ask:

What kind of support will my heart need as I open even more in the month ahead?

Closing Mantra for February

"I opened gently. I opened bravely.

What bloomed in me was real ~ and enough.

I honor the courage it took to soften."

March 1 - The Day of Gentle Becoming

A story of soft starts, honest beginnings, and learning that becoming is not about striving ~ it's about allowing

There once was a soul who believed change had to be dramatic.

A sudden shift. A bold decision. A before and after they could point to.

But one morning, they woke up and realized... something had shifted. Not all at once. Not loudly. But unmistakably.

They no longer felt the same pull toward what once drained them. They no longer shrank in the face of their own reflection.

There was no parade. Just a soft unfurling ~ like the first sprout pushing through soil.

"I'm becoming," they whispered. "Not all at once. But enough."

And for the first time, that was *plenty*.

March 1 carries the energy of 1 ~ the number of beginning, identity, and intention.

In Pisces' dreamy waters, this isn't the beginning of hustle. It's the beginning of *honest emergence.*

No more chasing. Just responding to what's already stirring inside you.

The archetype of the day is The Emerging One ~ the part of you no longer asleep, not yet rushing, but rising *with kindness.*

Today's symbols whisper renewal:

— A bud just breaking open, fragile and certain

— Green aventurine, crystal of new growth and self-trust

— The Fool card, stepping forward not in ignorance ~ but in faith

— A young fern, curled at the tip, unfolding slowly

This day brings healing to those who demand too much of themselves too soon. Who think they must leap when they're only just learning to stretch.

"You don't need to bloom yet," the day says.

"You only need to believe in your own slow unfolding."

And then, gently, a thought returns like a soft breeze from the past:

Do you remember February 1 ~ the Day of Soul Invitation?

This… is that quiet yes, now coming to life.

Later, the soul placed one hand over their lower belly, one over their chest, and said aloud:

"I welcome who I'm becoming. I don't need to rush it."

Being honest with yourself, ask:

— What feels new in me ~ not forced, just real?

— Where am I trying to "arrive" when I could simply "emerge"?

— How can I support the quiet version of me that's just starting to show up?

— What parts of me feel unfamiliar ~ but deeply true?

— What does it mean to grow in a way that doesn't need to be seen to be sacred?

They didn't need to prove anything. They only needed to *keep becoming*.

Sacred Actions: Start something today ~ not with effort, but with presence. Light a candle, take the first step, plant a seed. Whisper:

"Becoming is enough."

Symbolic Focus: The solar plexus, the back of the neck, the skin's edge in contact with air.

Your Mantra for Today ~

"I become gently. I grow with grace."

March 2 - The Day of Soul Patience

A story of trust in timing, inward tending, and learning that all growth ~ whether blooming or shedding ~ honors its own rhythm

There once was a soul who struggled to wait.

They wanted their healing to hurry. Their purpose to arrive. Their life to finally "start."

But nothing responded to pressure. No part of them opened on command.
And the more they forced, the more everything *froze*.

Until one day, while walking beneath a canopy of changing leaves ~ or perhaps beneath branches just beginning to bud ~ they noticed:

"Nature never rushes," they thought. "And yet... nothing is ever left undone."

And in that quiet truth, they stopped rushing their own becoming.

March 2 holds the vibration of 2, the number of balance, intuition, and sacred pacing. In the Northern Hemisphere, it's the tail-end of winter ~ a time of quiet roots preparing for bloom. In the Southern Hemisphere, it's the early pull of autumn ~ a time when nature teaches us how to let go *with rhythm, not resistance.*

Wherever you are, this day reminds you: You're not late. You're on time for *your* cycle.

The archetype of the day is The Rhythmic Soul ~ the one who honors their own seasons, who allows process to unfold, and who knows that patience isn't passivity ~ it's *participation in divine timing.*

Today's symbols speak with earthy grace:

— A seed underground, not visible ~ but profoundly alive

— Petrified wood, a crystal of ancient trust and slow wisdom

— The Seven of Pentacles, waiting not with frustration, but with quiet tending

— A koala or dormouse, resting in rhythm with light and season

This day brings healing for those who tie their worth to speed. For those who equate urgency with progress. For those who forget that both blossoming and shedding require time.

"Your season is not behind," the day says. "It is just different. And it is *yours*."

And in that breath, a question stirs like wind through trees:

What part of me is quietly growing ~ or quietly releasing ~ in perfect timing, even if no one sees it?

Later, the soul paused in the middle of their routine ~ not to quit, but to *notice*.

They breathed deeper. Moved slower. Did one task with care instead of speed.

Being honest with yourself, ask:

— What part of my life am I rushing that might actually require trust?

— What signs of quiet growth or transformation have I been overlooking?

— What does patience feel like in my body ~ and how can I practice it today?

They didn't need immediate answers. They needed to *wait well*.

Sacred Actions: Do something slowly on purpose today ~ eat, walk, stretch, or even speak. As you do, repeat:

"I trust the pace of my own becoming."

Symbolic Focus: The hands, the soles of the feet, the lungs during long exhales.

Your Mantra for Today ~

"I wait in wisdom. My rhythm is sacred."

March 3 - The Day of Inner Awakening

A story of quiet realization, soul-sourced energy, and the moment when something within stirs ~ not by force, but by readiness

There once was a soul who kept asking: *"When will it start?"*

They thought awakening would be loud. A bolt. A sign. A burning   bush.
They kept looking outward for the spark.

But one early morning, in the hush between night and day ~
Whether spring birds were just beginning to sing in the North,
or the scent of late summer was stretching into dusk in the South
~ They felt it.

Not outside. Inside.

A gentle warmth behind the ribs. A thought that didn't come from the mind, but from somewhere deeper:

"Something in me is waking up… and this time, it's *mine*."

No fanfare. Just truth. No push. Just presence.

March 3 is rich with the energy of 3 ~ the number of expression, awareness, and spiritual birth. In Pisces season, this energy doesn't scream ~ it *emerges* from the deep.

Today invites you into a personal *dawn*. The kind of awakening that feels like your soul stretching after a long sleep.

The archetype of the day is The Inner Dawnbreaker ~ the one who no longer waits for a call from the world, because they've heard the call from *within*.

Symbols for this day shimmer with gentle clarity:

— A single ray of morning light falling across a sleeping face

— Amethyst, for spiritual insight, intuitive clarity, and inner calm

— The Judgement card, not of shame ~ but of sacred awakening

— A hummingbird, hovering midair, sensing the sweetness that's always been there

This day brings healing for those who doubt their path because it doesn't match someone else's awakening. For those who've silenced their inner stirrings in the name of fitting in.

"You don't need to be loud to be real," the day whispers. "You just need to *listen*."

And like a gentle echo, a curiosity loop emerges from your past reflection:

Back on January 7 ~ the Day of the Hidden Ember ~ remember that quiet fire inside you? This is it now, flickering to life. You didn't miss it. It was waiting for you.

Later, the soul moved through their day not to change everything ~ but to notice what had already changed.

Being honest with yourself, ask:

— What am I sensing in myself that feels new, even if I don't fully understand it yet?

— Where have I already begun to shift, even if I haven't declared it out loud?

— What is trying to awaken in me ~ not from pressure, but from readiness?

They didn't try to name it. They just let it bloom.

Sacred Actions: Begin your day in silence ~ even for two minutes. Ask gently:

"What in me is ready to rise?"

Let the answer come not in words, but in energy.

Symbolic Focus: The crown of the head, the sternum, the breath just after waking.

Your Mantra for Today ~

"I awaken gently. I honor what rises within me."

March 4 - The Day of Brave Surrender

A story of choosing release with courage, letting go without defeat, and discovering that true strength often begins where control ends

There once was a soul who held on tightly.

To outcomes. To plans. To identities that once kept them safe ~ but now kept them small.

They called it responsibility. But under the surface, it was fear. Fear of who they might become without the familiar anchors.

One day, they stood at the edge of a decision ~ In the North, the wind still carried winter's breath; in the South, the golden hush of autumn had begun to fall across the fields.

And something in them whispered:

"You are brave enough to *not know* what comes next."

With hands trembling, they let go. Not because they stopped caring ~ but because they started *trusting*.

March 4 carries the energy of 4 ~ the number of foundation, grounded action, and inner strength. But today, that strength doesn't come from control ~ it comes from the courage to surrender what no longer serves your soul.

In Pisces, surrender is not defeat ~ it's a return. A sacred softening that makes space for what's next.

The archetype of the day is The Fearless Releaser ~ the one who chooses to set down the burden, not because it's easy, but because *it's time.*

Today's symbols hold gentle resolve:

— A candle burned low, its wax melted, its light still steady

— Selenite, for purification, clarity, and sacred letting go

— The Hanged Man, in suspension ~ not trapped, but choosing perspective

— A leaf on water, drifting freely, carried by something larger

This day brings healing for those who mistake control for safety. For those who feel guilty for letting go.

For those whose bravery has always looked like holding on ~ and are now learning that *bravery can look like release.*

"Letting go," the day says, "is not the end of the path. It's the clearing that reveals the next step."

And then, a familiar spark ~

Remember February 19, the Day of Soul Surrender? That wasn't a one-time release. This is the deeper layer ~ the surrender you choose *while still walking forward.*

Later, the soul placed a hand on their chest. Spoke a truth they had been holding back.

Or released a thought they could no longer carry.

Being honest with yourself, ask:

— What am I gripping that's actually keeping me from growing?

— Where am I pretending to be in control, when I'm really afraid to trust?

— What would it look like to surrender with strength ~ not shame?

They didn't collapse. They *rose* ~ lighter, clearer, freer.

Sacred Actions: Write a release note today ~ even if just one line. Burn it, bury it, or speak it aloud. Let yourself feel the moment when control transforms into trust.

Symbolic Focus: The hands, the belly, the space between the shoulder blades.

Your Mantra for Today ~

"I surrender with courage. I am safe in the letting go."

March 5 - The Day of Subtle Courage

A story of quiet bravery, small steps with soul, and honoring the inner strength it takes to keep going gently

There once was a soul who believed courage had to be loud.

They imagined roaring decisions, bold leaps, fearless declarations.

So when their courage looked more like showing up quietly, like saying "no" with a trembling voice, like getting out of bed on a heavy day ~ hey wondered, *"Does this even count?"*

But one afternoon, whether walking under late-winter skies in the North, or feeling the softened light of early autumn in the South, they stopped.

They looked back on the last few weeks ~ The tears they moved through. The truths they spoke. The boundaries they held, even shakily.

And they whispered:

"Maybe courage doesn't always shout. Maybe sometimes... it simply *stays*."

And in that moment, they stood a little taller ~ not from pride, but from *truth*.

March 5 carries the energy of 5 ~ the number of change, movement, and breakthrough. But Pisces reminds us: *not all movement looks like action*. Some of the bravest things happen *inwardly*, in silence, in softness.

The archetype of the day is The Quiet Brave ~ the one who keeps choosing themselves in small, sacred ways. The one whose tenderness is not a lack of strength ~ but the form strength sometimes takes when no one is watching.

Today's symbols hum with quiet depth:

— A dewdrop clinging to a leaf, holding on through morning chill

— Pink opal, for emotional healing, soft resilience, and spiritual gentleness

— The Page of Cups, openhearted, vulnerable, and deeply brave in expression

— A moth, drawn to light ~ small, steady, guided by instinct, not force

This day brings healing for those who've dismissed their strength because it didn't look like someone else's. For those who keep showing up without applause, who carry emotional weight and still choose kindness.

"Courage," the day says, "is sometimes just the decision to keep breathing when your soul feels tight."

And in the air ~ a gentle reminder:

Remember February 4 ~ the Day of Inner Friendship? The part of you learning to be kind to yourself? This is that same part now learning to be brave with you, too.

Later, the soul placed their hand on their heart. Took one deep, intentional breath. Did one thing they were afraid to do ~ even if it was simply *feeling* something fully.

Being honest with yourself, ask:

— Where have I been brave recently without giving myself credit?

— What act of courage is available to me today ~ even if no one else sees it?

— What would happen if I called my gentleness a form of strength?

No parade. Just presence.

Sacred Actions: Name one small act of bravery you've made this week. Write it down. Honor it. Then ask:

"What small, honest thing can I do today that my future self will thank me for?"

Symbolic Focus: The solar plexus, the tongue before speaking truth, the inhale before movement.

Your Mantra for Today ~

"My quiet courage is enough. I honor the strength in my softness."

March 6 - The Day of Restorative Honesty

A story of soft truth-telling, the kind that heals rather than harms, and the moment when honesty becomes a doorway ~ not a wall

There once was a soul who thought telling the truth meant hurting someone.

They'd been taught that honesty had edges ~ sharp, blunt, unforgiving. So they held it back. Filtered themselves. Swallowed words until silence became a habit.

But deep inside, they began to ache. Not from what they couldn't say ~ but from who they couldn't be.

Then one day, in a conversation that wasn't planned, in a moment that felt strangely tender, they said something simple and real:

"I'm not okay with this." Or maybe: "This matters to me." Or even just: *"Here's how I really feel."*

No anger. No explosion. Just truth ~ spoken from *wholeness*, not from fear.

And afterward… something shifted. Not just in the other person ~ but in *them*.

March 6 carries the energy of 6 ~ the number of heart-centered balance, relational healing, and honest communication. Pisces brings emotional depth and nuance, making this a day to practice truth that restores ~ not just reveals.

In the Northern Hemisphere, the air still holds winter's hush ~ a space for deep listening. In the Southern Hemisphere, early autumn begins to slow the tempo, asking what's essential and what can be released.

The archetype of the day is The Truth Healer ~ the one who tells the truth with love, who uses honesty not as a weapon but as a bridge, who knows that clarity is the soil where *real connection grows.*

Today's symbols reflect calm vulnerability:

— A mirror in soft light, showing not flaws ~ but presence

— Blue lace agate, stone of compassionate communication and emotional clarity

— The Queen of Swords, tempered wisdom, sharp but kind

— A dove, pausing midair, cooing gently ~ never needing to shout to be heard

This day brings healing for those who've feared honesty because of past harm ~ for those who've hidden their needs or truths to maintain peace.

"Truth," the day whispers, "is not the opposite of love. It's *how* love breathes."

And from within, a subtle echo from your past surfaces:

Remember February 6 ~ the Day of Emotional Honesty? Today you go one step further ~ not just naming what's real, but offering it with healing intention.

Later, the soul spoke a truth aloud ~ maybe in a journal, maybe in a text, maybe just to themselves ~ not to be loud, but to be *real.*

Being honest with yourself, ask:

— Where have I been holding back a truth to protect others ~ and is it costing me clarity?

— What would it sound like to speak honestly and kindly at the same time?

— What might I restore by letting my words reflect my heart ~ not my fear?

And as they wrote, something softened ~ and *aligned.*

Sacred Actions: Choose one small truth you've been holding back. Speak it gently ~ to yourself or someone else. Lead with love, not justification. Whisper:

"My truth deserves a place in this room."

Symbolic Focus: The throat, the lips before speaking, the pause after sharing something true.

Your Mantra for Today ~

"My truth is healing. I speak it with grace."

March 7 - The Day of Spiritual Integration

A story of weaving wisdom into daily life, carrying the sacred into the ordinary, and learning that enlightenment means nothing if it can't be lived

There once was a soul who collected wisdom like treasures.

Books, quotes, mantras, visions. They felt lit up by insight ~ grounded in meditation, expanded by meaning.

But when it came to conflict, dishes, fatigue, or disappointment ~ the wisdom disappeared. The peace dissolved.

They felt like two selves: the *spiritual* one, and the *everyday* one.

Until one day, while stirring soup or tying a shoelace or sitting in traffic, the soul remembered a truth they'd read long ago ~ Not as a concept, but as a *feeling*. Not to escape the moment, but to *be more present within it.*

"My spiritual life is not separate," they whispered. "It's here. In this."

And something clicked ~ not loudly, but completely.

March 7 carries the vibration of 7 ~ the number of spiritual alignment, soul wisdom, and sacred insight. Under the influence of Pisces, this becomes a day of integration: letting the mystical meet the mundane.

In the Northern Hemisphere, this could be the spiritual hush before spring's bloom. In the Southern Hemisphere, it might feel like a soft descent into inner stillness. Either way, today reminds you that your sacred self doesn't live far away ~ it lives *right here*.

The archetype of the day is The Embodied Mystic ~ the one who knows that the divine shows up in breath, in kindness, in the way we fold towels or offer a true smile. The one who carries the sacred *into life*.

Today's symbols radiate living presence:

—   A well-worn book with handwritten notes, truth made personal

—   Labradorite, for spiritual embodiment, intuition, and deeper layers of self

—   The Temperance card, blending spiritual and material into harmony

—   A hermit crab, carrying home and wisdom inside its body ~ always moving, always present

This day brings healing to those who think they're not "doing it right" unless they're perfectly spiritual. For those who seek transcendence but forget to *inhabit* their wisdom.

"You do not need to escape life to find the sacred," the day says. "You only need to *bring your soul with you* wherever you go."

And then, softly, a curiosity loop opens from past reflection:

Remember January 13 ~ the Day of Living Light?

That sacred flame within you wasn't meant for the mountaintop. It was meant for your daily life ~ right here, right now.

Later, the soul washed their face with presence. Or paused before a conversation. Or infused a task with awareness instead of resentment.

Being honest with yourself, ask:

— Where do I abandon my deeper wisdom in everyday life?

— What spiritual truths have I learned... but not yet lived?

— How can I carry the sacred with me today ~ in action, not just intention?

Their enlightenment didn't shine from above. It rose from *within.*

Sacred Actions: Choose one ordinary act today ~ like brushing your teeth, cooking, or answering a message ~ and do it with full soul presence. Let it become a ritual. Whisper:

"This is sacred too."

Symbolic Focus: The hands in motion, the feet on the floor, the breath during action.

Your Mantra for Today ~

"I live what I know. I carry the sacred into everything I do."

March 8 - The Day of Soft Power

A story of quiet strength, influence without force, and discovering that the most enduring kind of power is the one rooted in presence

There once was a soul who believed that to be powerful, they had to be loud.

They thought strength meant certainty. That leadership meant control. That to be seen, they had to push harder, speak bigger, shine brighter.

But one day, sitting in stillness ~ perhaps beneath the bare branches of late winter in the North, or among the slowly turning leaves of early autumn in the South ~ they noticed something else.

The breeze.

It moved trees without shouting. It shaped landscapes over time, not by dominance ~ but by *consistency*.

And the soul whispered:

"Maybe my power isn't in how I push. Maybe it's in how I *hold*."

They stopped trying to prove. And started simply *being*.

March 8 carries the number 8 ~ the number of inner authority, sustainable strength, and empowered alignment. In Pisces, it softens the sharp edges of power and transforms them into presence, flow, and *grace in action*.

This is not the day to dominate. It's the day to realize that you are powerful exactly as you are ~ even in stillness.

The archetype of the day is The Quiet Force ~ the one whose strength is felt, not shouted. The one who leads with calm, holds space with clarity, and trusts that influence doesn't require noise ~ it requires *alignment*.

Today's symbols radiate subtle strength:

— A river cutting through stone, soft yet undeniable

— Hematite, grounding and protective, a stone of magnetic balance

— The Strength card, not of battle, but of quiet mastery

— A panther, moving silently, eyes steady ~ confident without spectacle

This day brings healing for those who have been told their softness makes them small. For those who equate volume with visibility. For those who long to stand firm *without having to fight*.

"Power," the day says, "does not require armor. It only requires truth."

And like a thread woven from past to present:

Remember February 5 ~ the Day of Soul Gentleness? That same softness is now revealing its power. What once protected you now guides you.

Later, the soul paused before reacting. They responded with clarity instead of heat. They stood in their center ~ and realized they didn't need to raise their voice to be heard.

Being honest with yourself, ask:

— Where have I confused dominance with true power?

— What quiet strength in me is asking to lead today?

— How can I influence without controlling ~ and stay rooted in my truth?

They felt no need to prove. Only to *embody*.

Sacred Actions: Choose one moment today to lead or respond with grounded calm ~ especially where you'd normally overextend or defend. Whisper:

"My presence is enough."

Symbolic Focus: The spine, the gaze, the breath during stillness.

Your Mantra for Today ~

"My power is soft, steady, and sure."

March 9 - The Day of Unfolding Trust

A story of surrendering control, leaning into the unknown, and letting life hold you ~ even when the next step isn't clear

There once was a soul who only felt safe when they had a plan.

They organized, predicted, prepared. They checked weather forecasts and backup routes, read between the lines, made sure every risk was covered.

And still… life surprised them.

But one afternoon ~ whether in the North, where the final frost had yet to melt, or in the South, where dusk arrived a little earlier ~ they stood at a threshold.

They didn't know what came next. And for once, instead of forcing clarity, they paused.

They felt their breath. They felt the ground. They looked up, and said:

"I don't know what's ahead… but I trust what's holding me now."

It wasn't certainty. It was *peace*.

March 9 carries the energy of 9 ~ the number of wisdom, culmination, and spiritual perspective. In the intuitive waters of Pisces, this becomes a day of trust without proof ~ a sacred release into *becoming without needing to know the outcome.*

Today doesn't ask you to plan. It asks you to *lean* ~ into something larger, deeper, quieter than control.

The archetype of the day is The Soul Leaper ~ the one who doesn't need every answer to take a step.

The one who knows that the net often appears *after* the leap ~ not before.

Today's symbols invite grounded faith:

— Two open hands, not empty ~ but *ready*

— Aquamarine, for courage, surrender, and emotional trust

— The Fool card, not naive ~ but free, heart-first

— A bridge fading into mist, walked not by sight, but by knowing

This day brings healing for those who've relied on control to feel safe. For those who've withheld decisions, dreams, or joy because the outcome couldn't be guaranteed.

"You don't have to know what's next," the day says. "You only have to trust who you are as you take the next step."

And softly, a reflection loop glimmers:

Remember March 1 ~ the Day of Gentle Becoming? That inner spark? Today is when you trust it enough to follow where it leads.

Later, the soul let one question go unanswered. They moved toward what felt right, even if it wasn't "certain." They made peace with not knowing ~ and in that peace, they felt *held.*

Being honest with yourself, ask:

— What am I waiting to know before I act ~ and do I really need to know it yet?

— Where is life asking me to soften, trust, and take one small step?

— What does trust feel like in my body ~ and how can I return to it today?

They didn't control the unfolding.

They chose to *unfold with it.*

Sacred Actions: Do something today without a guaranteed outcome ~ reach out, say yes, make a start. Whisper:

"I trust myself. I trust the unfolding."

Symbolic Focus: The palms, the ankles before a step, the solar plexus during stillness.

Your Mantra for Today ~

"I let go of control. I lean into trust."

March 10 ~ The Day of Soul and Remembering

A story of inner return, quiet recognition, and the moment when you realize you've always known ~ you just forgot to listen

There once was a soul who searched far and wide for truth.

They read books. Asked teachers. Followed trends. They gathered answers like puzzle pieces, but the image never felt complete.

Until one morning ~ maybe while watching the final snow melt in the North, or while sensing the deeper hush of approaching autumn in the South ~ they stopped searching.

They went quiet. Not because they gave up ~ but because something within whispered:

"You already know. You've always known."

And in that breath, what had once felt distant... returned.

It wasn't a new idea. It was an *old truth*, finally remembered.

March 10 carries the energy of 1 (1 + 0), a number of identity, beginning, and sacred selfhood. In Pisces season, it becomes an invitation to not reinvent ~ but to return. To reconnect with the knowing you were born with.

This isn't about discovering a new path. It's about realizing you've been on it all along ~ and now, you're ready to walk it with clarity.

The archetype of the day is The Remembering Soul ~ the one who gathers lost pieces, not to become something else, but to reclaim who they've always been beneath the noise.

Today's symbols evoke gentle clarity:

— A compass held over the heart, slowly spinning into place

— Celestite, a crystal of divine remembrance and soul reconnection

— The Six of Cups, memories, roots, and inner child integration

— A sea turtle, returning home to where life began ~ steady, ancient, sure

This day brings healing for those who've felt lost in comparison, distraction, or spiritual amnesia. For those who've tried so hard to become "better" that they forgot they were already *whole*.

"This isn't a search," the day says. "It's a homecoming."

And softly, a loop stirs from earlier pages:

Remember February 9 ~ the Day of Remembered Wholeness?

Today is not a repeat ~ it is the deeper layer of that return. This time, you don't just remember... you live it.

Later, the soul revisited a childhood memory, a journal entry, or a dream that never quite faded. They didn't overanalyze it. They *felt* it ~ and knew it meant something real.

Being honest with yourself, ask:

— What part of me have I always known ~ even when I forgot?

— What do I deeply remember when I stop seeking and start listening?

— How can I let that soul truth guide my next step today?

They stopped chasing clarity. And let it *rise from within.*

Sacred Actions: Find one old object ~ a photo, a note, a favorite childhood item. Sit with it. Ask:

"What part of me does this help me remember?"

Symbolic Focus: The heart center, the back of the neck, the breath during stillness.

Your Mantra for Today ~

"I remember who I am. I carry my truth home."

March 11 - The Day of Inner Stewardship

A story of protecting what matters, nurturing the self with care, and realizing that your energy is a sacred resource ~ not for everyone, not for everything

There once was a soul who gave without limit.

Their time. Their presence. Their energy ~ freely offered, endlessly spent.

They thought that love meant availability. That kindness meant always saying yes. But over time, they grew tired. Not the kind of tired sleep could fix ~ but the kind that comes from *self-neglect disguised as generosity.*

Then one day, as the days subtly lengthened in the North, or the shadows grew softer in the South, they felt it in their bones:

"I am responsible for this ~ my energy, my space, my sacred self."

And in that moment, they didn't shut the world out. They simply chose what would *remain in.*

March 11 holds the energy of 2 (1 + 1), the number of balance, boundary, and relational care. Pisces softens it, bringing empathy ~ but today is not about pouring endlessly into others. It's about stewarding your soul with intention.

This is a day for choosing where your energy goes ~ and where it returns to you. A day for protecting what matters without guilt.

The archetype of the day is The Soul Steward ~ the one who tends to their inner garden with vigilance and gentleness alike. The one who gives from overflow, not depletion.

Today's symbols offer strength with softness:

—   A walled sanctuary filled with growing things, peaceful and protected

—   Black tourmaline, for energetic boundaries and grounded strength

—   The Nine of Pentacles, self-possession, abundance, and peaceful protection

—   A badger, unassuming but fiercely clear ~ gentle until pushed too far

This day brings healing to those who've overextended for love, for approval, or from a belief that being needed is the same as being valued.

"You are not selfish for tending to your energy," the day says. "You are *wise*."

And subtly, a curiosity loop draws you back:

Remember February 8 ~ the Day of Soft Boundaries? That was the *invitation*. Today is the *embodiment*. Now, you're not just saying no ~ you're saying yes to *yourself*.

Later, the soul reviewed their schedule, their habits, their relationships ~ not with blame, but with *discernment*.

Being honest with yourself, ask:

— Where am I giving out of obligation instead of joy?

— What part of my life needs stronger stewardship ~ and how can I begin today?

— What would it feel like to live in a way that protects my peace before I lose it?

Their generosity didn't disappear. It just became *rooted*.

Sacred Actions: Say no to one thing today ~ even if it's small. Then choose one thing that deeply nourishes your energy. Whisper:

"I honor the energy that sustains me."

Symbolic Focus: The root chakra, the hands drawn inward, the exhale after a boundary is set.

Your Mantra for Today ~

"I tend to myself with wisdom and care."

March 12 - The Day of Soul Intuition

A story of deep knowing, quiet signals, and remembering that your inner compass has always pointed true ~ if only you'll pause to listen

There once was a soul who doubted themselves often.

They second-guessed. Asked for signs. Looked outside for direction ~ even when something inside whispered softly.

But they'd learned not to trust that whisper. Not because it had been wrong... but because the world had been *louder*.

Then one evening ~ with the Northern Hemisphere cloaked in still-cold skies, and the Southern Hemisphere tinged with early twilight winds ~ the soul felt it again.

Not a voice. Not a vision. Just a pull. A nudge. A knowing.

"Go this way," it said. Not because it made sense. But because it made *truth*.

And this time... they listened.

March 12 carries the number 3 (1 + 2), the number of expression, alignment, and divine flow. But in Pisces, that expression is not loud or performative ~ it's *intuitive*. It rises from the soul, not the surface.

Today, you are reminded: Your intuition isn't vague. It's just quiet. And when you slow down enough to feel it, it becomes your most trustworthy guide.

The archetype of the day is The Inner Oracle ~ the one who no longer waits for signs from the outside world, because they've learned to *interpret the signs within*.

Today's symbols are subtle and sacred:

— A spiral shell, holding sound and silence in equal measure

— Moonstone, crystal of inner vision, cycles, and soul-tuned insight

— The High Priestess, keeper of hidden truths and sacred timing

— An owl, turning its head without effort, seeing in all directions

This day brings healing for those who've overridden their intuition in favor of logic, who've shamed their inner voice for not being louder, or who've been told that "gut feelings" aren't real.

"You don't need to explain your knowing," the day whispers.

"You only need to *honor it*."

And softly, a memory flows in like tide to shore:

*Back on February 11 ~ the Day of Quiet Knowing ~ your soul offered you truth without noise. Today, that same truth invites you to *follow it*.

Later, the soul made a choice ~ not the most rational one, not the easiest ~ but the one that *felt right* in their bones.

Being honest with yourself, ask:

— What decision or direction feels aligned ~ even if I can't explain why?

— Where in my body do I feel "yes"? Where do I feel "no"?

— What happens when I trust my knowing before I need proof?

No analysis. Just attunement.

Sacred Actions: Ask yourself one question aloud today ~ then sit in silence and feel the first answer that arises. Trust it. Act from it. Whisper:

"I hear myself. I trust my knowing."

Symbolic Focus: The third eye, the space beneath the navel, the breath between question and answer.

Your Mantra for Today ~

"My soul knows the way. I listen, and I follow."

March 13 - The Day of Grounded Magic

A story of everyday wonder, real-world enchantment, and the realization that the mystical isn't separate from your life ~ it's hidden inside it

There once was a soul who thought magic had to be extraordinary.

They looked for signs in the sky, for rituals in faraway places, for meaning that arrived only through ceremony.

They lit candles. Spoke mantras. Waited for a spark.

But one morning ~ maybe beneath the last breath of frost in the North, or during a golden walk through early autumn light in the South ~ they looked down.

There, in the curve of a leaf, the rhythm of their breath, the pattern of chipped paint on a wall… was magic.

"It's always been here," they thought. "It's not something I summon. It's something I *see*."

March 13 carries the energy of 4 (1 + 3), the number of structure, presence, and embodiment. Pisces brings dreams and wonder ~ but today reminds you that magic doesn't just float above you… it *lives in your feet.*

This is a day for seeing the sacred in the simple. For letting mystery meet *daily life.* For living your magic *out loud* ~ not just in ritual, but in routine.

The archetype of the day is The Everyday Mystic ~ the one who brews tea like a spell, speaks kindly like a prayer, and finds divinity not only in altars, but in eye contact, cracked sidewalks, and cooking dinner.

Today's symbols shimmer gently through the mundane:

— A stone with a glittering core, found by chance on a morning walk

— Clear quartz, amplifying what's already present ~ no additions needed

— The Magician card, grounding divine energy through real-world hands

— A crow, collecting shiny things, reminding us that symbols are everywhere

This day brings healing for those who separate their spiritual life from their real life. For those who feel they must "leave the world" to find peace ~ or that wonder is reserved only for "special" moments.

"Magic is not rare," the day says. "It is *revealed* by presence."

And then, with a wink from the past:

Remember January 22 ~ the Day of Living Symbols?

Today's enchantment grows from that same insight: The world is always speaking. Are you present enough to listen?

Later, the soul stirred their coffee like a ritual. Lit a candle ~ not for a spell, but for light. And as they did, they felt *connected*.

Being honest with yourself, ask:

— What if every part of my day is sacred ~ if I let it be?

— Where have I dismissed wonder because it felt too ordinary?

— How can I root my spirituality more deeply into my real life today?

No more separating magic from reality. Just *living in both*.

Sacred Actions: Take one ordinary action ~ walking, cleaning, cooking ~ and do it as a *spell*. Say aloud:

"This, too, is sacred. I create meaning by being present."

Symbolic Focus: The soles of the feet, the hands in motion, the eyes when they soften.

Your Mantra for Today ~

"My magic lives in what I do with love."

March 14 ~ The Day of Gentle Insight

A story of wisdom arriving like a breeze, not a thunderclap ~ and learning to value the quiet truths that change everything

There once was a soul who waited for clarity to strike.

They thought insight came in flashes. That big answers required big moments. That wisdom had to arrive with lightning, not stillness.

But one day ~ whether wrapped in the grey-blue hush of late Northern winter, or the golden softness of the Southern autumn sun ~ they noticed something different.

They were sipping tea. Watching dust dance in sunlight. Not seeking, just *being*.

And then it came ~ Not a solution, but an understanding. Not an answer, but a shift.

"This," the soul thought, "is wisdom… arriving without effort."

It didn't demand anything. It just *landed* ~ like a petal on still water.

March 14 carries the number 5 (1 + 4), often tied to movement, change, and expansion. But under Pisces' gentle current, this day speaks of a softer shift ~ the kind of change that *emerges through awareness, not action.*

Today, you are invited to let your insights come quietly ~ to trust the subtle way your soul speaks when you're not forcing, fixing, or chasing.

The archetype of the day is The Listening Heart ~ the part of you that receives truth as a whisper, not a warning. The part of you that understands some of the deepest revelations are *felt before they're spoken.*

Today's symbols are subtle but luminous:

— A single feather drifting through sunlight, barely moving

— Blue calcite, for soft insight, emotional clarity, and inner translation

— The Page of Swords, curious, open, learning not just with mind ~ but with presence

— A dragonfly, hovering ~ seeing all, disturbing nothing

This day brings healing for those who believe growth must be loud or painful. For those who overlook the wisdom in slow realizations, or who think insight only counts when it feels "big."

"You don't need to hunt truth," the day whispers. "You only need to *receive it.*"

And gently, a thread of memory ripples forward:

Remember March 3 ~ the Day of Inner Awakening?

This is the follow-up echo: That awakening is now speaking to you… in a softer language. Are you still listening?

Later, the soul sat by a window. Or walked without headphones. Or closed their eyes in a quiet room ~ not to meditate, but to *notice*.

Being honest with yourself, ask:

— What quiet realizations have been visiting me lately, just beneath the surface?

— Where might I find clarity not by thinking more ~ but by softening?

— How can I honor gentle wisdom without needing to dramatize or prove it?

There were no conclusions. Only clarity ~ quiet, kind, and complete.

Sacred Actions: Let part of your day be wordless. Listen without analysis. Trust the feeling that rises without needing to name it. Whisper:

"Truth arrives when I make space."

Symbolic Focus: The temples, the fingertips, the heart before reaction.

Your Mantra for Today ~

"I receive my wisdom gently. I trust the quiet truth."

March 15 - The Day of Clear Boundaries

A story of self-honoring, energetic clarity, and learning that saying no can be the most sacred yes to yourself

There once was a soul who said yes too often.

They agreed to things that didn't feel right. They stayed in conversations that drained them. They held space for others even when they had none left for themselves.

They called it kindness. But it was exhaustion in disguise.

Then one day ~ perhaps in the lingering cool of late winter in the North, or as the first leaves fell in the South ~ they felt a different kind of knowing rise:

"This isn't sustainable. And I don't have to apologize for protecting my energy."

So the soul said no. Softly. Clearly. And to their surprise ~ the world didn't end.

They just found *space to breathe again.*

March 15 carries the energy of 6 (1 + 5), a number of balance, harmony, and relational healing. Pisces softens and expands your empathy ~ but today reminds you that real empathy includes *you.*

This isn't about pushing people away. It's about inviting yourself back in by drawing the line where your energy ends and someone else's begins.

The archetype of the day is The Loving Gatekeeper ~ the part of you that can be kind and clear at the same time. The one who protects your sacred space without guilt.

Today's symbols radiate protection and peace:

— A line drawn in soft sand, held with love

— Obsidian, for energetic shielding and truth-aligned choices

— The Two of Swords, a moment of decision, a return to self

— A hedgehog, curled up, not to hide ~ but to care for what's tender within

This day brings healing for those who overextend, say yes out of fear, or have been conditioned to equate boundaries with rejection.

"Boundaries," the day says, "are not walls. They are doors you choose when ~ and *if* ~ to open."

And gently, a thread connects back:

Remember February 23 ~ the Day of Rooted Sensitivity?

That sensitivity now becomes discernment. Today, you learn to stand in it ~ not shrink from it.

Later, the soul paused before replying. Or closed a tab. Or said, "Not today." And for the first time, that choice felt like *care*, not cruelty.

Being honest with yourself, ask:

— What boundary have I been avoiding because I fear disappointing someone?

— Where does my body say "no" before my mouth does?

— How can I hold my boundaries with love, not just for others ~ but for me?

And as they did, they felt something shift ~ from depletion to *dignity*.

Sacred Actions: Name one boundary you've been hesitant to set. Practice stating it aloud, softly but clearly. Whisper:
"This protects my peace ~ and honors my truth."

Symbolic Focus: The jaw, the solar plexus, the back body when upright.

Your Mantra for Today ~

"My boundaries are clear. My care includes me."

March 16 - The Day of Quiet Resilience

A story of strength without spectacle, endurance without ego, and the sacred power of those who bend ~ but do not break

There once was a soul who didn't realize how strong they were.

They thought resilience meant showing no pain. They thought it looked like pushing through, never faltering, always "fine."

But the truth was… they had weathered storms. They had sat with grief without turning away. They had stood again, even when their heart was still shaking.

One day ~ beneath skies holding the final breath of winter in the North, or the soft rustle of early fall in the South ~ they didn't do anything grand.

They just kept going. And this time, they *noticed* what that really meant.

"This," the soul whispered, "is resilience. Quiet. Steady. Sacred."

March 16 carries the energy of 7 (1 + 6), a number of spiritual strength, inner reflection, and soul endurance. In Pisces' soft waters, this isn't about showing the world how strong you are. It's about *knowing it for yourself.*

Today honors the kind of strength that doesn't perform ~ the kind that heals slowly, walks softly, and never stops rising, no matter how many times it falls.

The archetype of the day is The Silent Pillar ~ the one whose stability comes from deep inner work, not outer display. The one who bends in the wind, but roots deeper each time.

Today's symbols are ancient and strong:

— A stone path partially grown over, still present, still guiding

— Jasper, a stone of grounded endurance and embodied strength

— The Nine of Wands, worn but wise, resilient without resistance

— A willow tree, swaying but never uprooted ~ flexible and fierce

This day brings healing for those who've minimized their strength because it wasn't flashy. For those who've survived quietly. For those who've felt invisible while enduring *everything.*

"You don't have to prove your strength," the day says. "You've *lived* it."

And as you take this in, a memory ripples forward:

Remember February 13 ~ the Day of Embodied Grace?

That was strength in motion. Today, it becomes your foundation ~ not loud, but unshakable.

Later, the soul looked in the mirror. Not to check their reflection ~ but to *recognize it*. To see the story of everything they'd made it through… and still chose to love.

Being honest with yourself, ask:

— What have I survived that I've never honored fully?

— Where does my quiet resilience live ~ in routine, in choice, in softness?

— How can I remind myself today: I am strong, even when I'm still healing?

They didn't need permission to be powerful. They simply *remembered.*

Sacred Actions: Name one moment of quiet strength from your past. Say it aloud. Thank yourself for enduring it ~ not with pressure, but with awe. Whisper:

"I bend. I don't break. I rise."

Symbolic Focus: The spine, the heels, the center of the palms when open.

Your Mantra for Today ~

"My strength is steady. My resilience is sacred."

March 17 - The Day of Wholehearted Expression

A story of speaking from the soul, creating without apology, and remembering that your voice is not just valid ~ it's vital

There once was a soul who silenced themselves.

Not because they had nothing to say. But because they feared it would be too much ~ or not enough. Too messy, too emotional, too different.

They swallowed ideas. Smoothed out edges. Waited for the "right" time to share who they were.

But one day ~ under a sky beginning to warm in the Northern Hemisphere, or as golden leaves fell softly in the Southern Hemisphere ~ they felt it rise.

A sentence. A truth. A piece of art. A story. A sound.

It came from the chest, not the mind. It came *whole*.

"This is me," they whispered. "And I don't need to perfect it ~ only to *release* it."

March 17 carries the energy of 8 (1 + 7), a number of personal power, voice, and energetic flow. Under the Piscean influence, this power isn't performance ~ it's *presence*. The power to express your truth with heart, not armor.

Today invites you to express not just what's expected ~ but what's *real*. To give your words, your creativity, your voice space to move freely.

The archetype of the day is The Soul Speaker ~ the one who creates from within, who shares because it heals, and who knows that expression is not ego ~ it's embodiment.

Today's symbols pulse with authenticity:

— A paintbrush dipped in water, colors blurring but vibrant

— Carnelian, for creative courage, voice activation, and vitality

— The Knight of Wands, inspired action fueled by passion

— A parrot, bright and bold ~ repeating nothing, expressing everything

This day brings healing for those who've withheld expression out of fear of judgment, rejection, or ridicule. For those who learned to speak in ways that pleased others ~ and forgot what *their own voice* sounded like.

"You are not too much," the day says. "You are *meant* to be heard."

And then ~ a meaningful return echoes gently:

Remember January 3 ~ the Day of Soul Truth?

That truth is now ready to speak ~ not privately, but out loud. This is your moment of integration through voice.

Later, the soul wrote a poem. Sang out loud. Spoke an honest sentence in a room where they once felt small.

Being honest with yourself, ask:

— What do I want to express that I've been afraid to say or show?

— Where have I been filtering myself ~ and why?

— What would change if I expressed my soul without shrinking or rushing?

They didn't perform. They *released.*

Sacred Actions: Express something today ~ art, words, sound, gesture ~ without editing it for others. Say:

"This is me.

This is honest.

This is enough."

Symbolic Focus: The throat, the hands, the pulse behind the ribs when you speak.

Your Mantra for Today ~

"I express with courage. I share from the soul."

March 18 - The Day of Inner Balance

A story of returning to center, honoring both shadow and light, and finding peace not in perfection ~ but in presence

There once was a soul who lived in extremes.

All or nothing. On or off. Productive or still. Strong or soft. They swung between poles, chasing "enough," never quite landing in themselves.

They believed balance meant achieving the perfect mix ~ a formula, a checklist, a static state of harmony.

But one afternoon ~ beneath lengthening skies in the Northern Hemisphere, or earlier sunsets in the Southern Hemisphere ~ they paused.

In that moment, nothing was finished. Nothing was perfect. But they were breathing. Grounded. Present.

And it dawned:

"Balance isn't a goal I hit. It's the way I come home to myself... again and again."

March 18 carries the energy of 9 (1 + 8), the number of inner mastery, integration, and closure. Under Pisces' mystical tide, today invites you to see balance as a *felt experience*, not a fixed outcome.

This is not the balance of scheduling or symmetry ~ it's soul balance. It lives in your breath, your awareness, your gentle re-centering.

The archetype of the day is The Inner Harmonizer ~ the one who knows that life is always in motion, and balance is not stillness... it's *response*. A dynamic, conscious act of self-honoring.

Today's symbols feel steady and fluid:

— A set of scales moving slightly in breeze, never locked, always adjusting

— Lepidolite, for emotional regulation, nervous system calm, and clarity

— The Justice card, not of punishment ~ but of truth and energetic equilibrium

— A crane, pausing mid-step in shallow water ~ poised, attentive, whole

This day brings healing for those who feel "off" unless everything is under control. For those who burn out trying to maintain perfection instead of embracing presence.

"Balance," the day says, "isn't the absence of motion. It's the return to your center ~ again and again."

And quietly, a previous thread returns to meet you:

Remember February 22 ~ the Day of Sacred Alignment?

That foundation now deepens. Today, you live the alignment not through rigidity, but through rhythm.

Later, the soul took three deep breaths before answering a message. They walked a little slower. They didn't need to "fix" themselves ~ they simply *adjusted*.

Being honest with yourself, ask:

— Where have I been seeking external balance instead of inner grounding?

— What signs tell me I'm off-center ~ and how can I respond with compassion, not control?

— What helps me return to myself when the world feels chaotic?

They weren't balanced forever. They just returned ~ *again and again*.

Sacred Actions: Pause once today ~ mid-task, mid-thought, mid-conversation ~ and gently ask:

"What would balance look like in this moment?"

Follow it. Even if only for a breath.

Symbolic Focus: The spine, the breath between inhale and exhale, the feet grounded evenly.

Your Mantra for Today ~

"Balance is not a state. It is my return to center."

March 19 - The Day of Sacred Timing

A story of divine pace, patient unfolding, and the deep wisdom that arises when you realize ~ not everything beautiful happens fast

There once was a soul who rushed through everything.

Not out of carelessness ~ but fear. Fear of missing out. Fear of falling behind. Fear that life might leave without them if they didn't keep up.

They pushed. They anticipated. They questioned the delays and cursed the detours.

But one twilight ~ as spring quietly approached in the Northern Hemisphere, and the Southern Hemisphere leaned gently into autumn's stillness ~ they noticed something.

A blossom had opened. Not when predicted. Not on schedule. But when it was *ready*.

"Maybe timing isn't about control," the soul whispered. "Maybe it's about trust."

March 19 carries the number 1 (1 + 9 = 10 → 1), a number of initiation, choice, and new beginnings. But under Pisces' contemplative tide, that beginning isn't rushed ~ it is rooted in timing that honors your soul's rhythm.

This is the day to stop forcing and start *flowing* ~ not out of passivity, but out of profound respect for what is *becoming*.

The archetype of the day is The Divine Paced One ~ the soul who honors pauses as much as starts, who trusts delay as sacred preparation, and who lives attuned to their own readiness, not society's race.

Today's symbols feel timeless and deep:

— An hourglass half-filled, light streaming through each falling grain

— Rhodochrosite, for compassion, soul trust, and heart-centered pacing

— The Wheel of Fortune, a reminder that seasons ~ and shifts ~ unfold in their own time

— A moonflower, blooming only at night, in its own quiet rhythm

This day brings healing to those who equate pace with purpose. For those who have felt "behind" in life, or have rushed healing, growth, or relationships from a place of fear.

"What's meant for you," the day says, "doesn't arrive faster when you rush ~ it arrives clearer when you're *ready*."

And from earlier reflections, a quiet thread reappears:

Remember March 2 ~ the Day of Soul Patience?

That patience has matured. Today, it becomes not just a waiting, but a knowing ~ that timing is sacred because you are sacred.

Later, the soul released one deadline ~ mentally, emotionally, spiritually. Not out of surrender. But sovereignty. They stopped sprinting. And felt time *meet* them, not outrun them.

Being honest with yourself, ask:

— Where have I been rushing what's meant to unfold?

— What's happening in perfect time ~ even if I don't see the full picture yet?

— How might my soul feel if I trusted that everything is arriving on time?*

They didn't lose momentum. They *reclaimed alignment.*

Sacred Actions: Choose one area of your life today to slow down. Take your hand off the clock. Say aloud:

"I trust the timing of my soul."

Symbolic Focus: The breath during pauses, the pulse in stillness, the center of the chest when you surrender time.

Your Mantra for Today ~

"I move in sacred time. I trust what is ripening in me."

March 20 - The Day of Equinox and Illumination

A story of cosmic balance, seasonal transition, and the sacred clarity that arrives when day and night stand equal ~ within you, and around you

There once was a soul who lived in contrast.

They loved the light but feared the dark. Chased growth but rejected rest. Praised beginnings and resisted endings.

They saw life in halves ~ opposites to be managed, not embraced.

But one day ~ as the Earth reached its perfect tilt ~ equal light and dark across both hemispheres, something shifted. In the North, winter gave way to spring. In the South, summer bowed to autumn. It was not chaos. It was *balance*.

And the soul realized:

"Maybe I don't need to choose one or the other. Maybe I'm meant to hold *both*."

March 20 is the March Equinox, a sacred pivot point when Earth's axis aligns just so ~ creating equal day and night, shadow and light, inhale and exhale.

It carries the numerological essence of 2 (2 + 0), the number of relationship, duality, and integration.

Today is not about either/or ~ it's about both/and. Not light *versus* shadow, but light *through* shadow. Not full bloom *or* full release ~ but the dance that makes both possible.

The archetype of the day is The Soul Balancer ~ the one who walks the line between worlds, who lives the paradox, who knows that wholeness requires all parts ~ even the ones we once hid.

Today's symbols hold dual beauty:

— A circle split evenly between gold and midnight blue, neither overpowering the other

— Sunstone + Moonstone, carried together ~ the sacred masculine and feminine in harmony

— A snake shedding skin under full sun, grounded in both rebirth and release

This day brings healing to those who feel fragmented. For those who've been taught to prefer progress over pause, clarity over confusion, love over grief ~ instead of holding all as sacred.

"This is not a war between light and dark," the day says. "This is a *reunion*. Within you. Around you. Always." And in that still, eternal balance ~ a thread is drawn:

Remember January 1 ~ the Day of Sacred Thresholds?

That was the door. Today, you step through it ~ carrying every part of yourself, into deeper light.

Later, the soul stood in both shadow and sun. Felt grief and gratitude. Felt tender and strong. And for once, they didn't need to resolve the tension.

They *honored it.*

Being honest with yourself, ask:

— Where have I split myself into "light" and "dark" ~ and what wants to be united?

— What seasonal energy is rising in me ~ and what is falling away?

— How can I live this day as a ceremony of inner balance and outer beauty?

They became the equinox. *They didn't just witness the balance ~ they became it.*

Sacred Actions: Create a small equinox ritual today ~ light a candle and sit in natural light or darkness. Reflect on what is rising and what is resting in your life. Whisper:

"I carry both light and shadow. I am whole."

Symbolic Focus: The left and right sides of the body, the breath in balance, the space between inhale and exhale.

Your Mantra for Today ~

"I honor the light. I honor the dark. I live in sacred balance."

March 21 - The Day of Soul Momentum

A story of aligned movement, courageous direction, and the sacred energy that awakens when your inner and outer life move together

There once was a soul who longed to move forward.

They had dreams, ideas, desires ~ but every time they tried to begin, something felt... stuck. They waited for motivation. They waited for clarity. They waited for permission.

Then, one morning ~ after the balance of the equinox had passed ~ the world itself shifted. In the Northern Hemisphere, buds unfurled, warmth returned. In the Southern Hemisphere, winds cooled and leaves began to fall.

And something inside the soul echoed that shift.

"It's time," they whispered. Not to rush ~ but to *begin*.

This wasn't force. It was *momentum* ~ soul-aligned, purpose-guided, season-supported.

March 21 carries the energy of 3 (2 + 1), the number of movement, expression, and creation. As the first *full day* after the

Equinox, it signals a new phase ~ both in the outer world and in your inner unfolding.

Whether you're entering spring's beginning or autumn's descent, this day invites forward motion that is rooted ~ not frantic. A momentum that comes from within, not from pressure.

The archetype of the day is The Soul Archer ~ the one who doesn't just aim wildly, but pulls the bowstring back with *intention*, releasing their next steps with trust and direction.

Today's symbols hum with motion and clarity:

— An arrow in mid-flight, not just launched ~ but *guided*

— Citrine, for confident action, creative flow, and purposeful expansion

— The Chariot card, momentum through alignment ~ not effort alone

— A salmon leaping upstream, instinct-led, resilient, unwavering

This day brings healing for those who doubt their timing, who hesitate at the threshold, or who wait for certainty before allowing themselves to move. For those who've prepared quietly ~ and are now *ready to begin.*

"You don't need to rush," the day says. "You only need to *move in the direction of your becoming.*"

And in that forward step, a reflection gently loops back:

Remember January 11 ~ the Day of Soul Momentum's Seed?

That intention planted in stillness? Today, it begins to grow legs. Not perfectly. But powerfully.

Later, the soul wrote one email. Made one decision. Took one step ~ not as a performance, but as *alignment in action.*

Being honest with yourself, ask:

— What momentum is rising in me ~ and how can I honor it?

— What's one move I can make today that says, "I trust where I'm headed"?

— What would change if I stopped waiting and started walking?

They didn't leap off cliffs. They *leaned into direction* ~ and felt life respond.

Sacred Actions: Take one aligned action today. No pressure. Just movement. Ask:

"What does my soul want to move toward?"

Then begin ~ even if just one breath forward.

Symbolic Focus: The feet in motion, the space behind the sternum, the back of the shoulders.

Your Mantra for Today ~

"I move with purpose. My momentum is sacred."

March 22 - The Day of Sacred Listening

A story of quiet attention, deep presence, and the healing that happens when we stop waiting to respond ~ and start truly hearing

There once was a soul who longed to be heard.

They spoke from the heart ~ but felt unheard. They gave advice ~ but didn't feel seen. They searched for deeper connection, but conversation always felt… shallow.

One day ~ while walking through blooming spring air in the North, or under falling leaves in the South ~ the soul sat beside a tree and simply listened.

Not to respond. Not to fix. Just to *receive*.

The breeze rustled. The earth hummed. And something inside softened.

"This," they realized, "is how I wish to be listened to… and how I'll begin listening to the world."

March 22 carries the energy of 4 (2 + 2), the number of foundation, presence, and grounding. With Pisces offering emotional depth and intuitive flow, this day becomes a sacred portal for deep, compassionate listening.

Not just hearing sounds ~ but attuning to *truth beneath words*.

The archetype of the day is The Soul Listener ~ the one who listens with their whole body, who honors silence as part of the conversation, and who knows that true connection begins with *presence*, not performance.

Today's symbols are soft and resonant:

— A bowl of still water, catching every vibration

— Chrysocolla, stone of compassionate communication and heartfelt listening

— The Queen of Cups, openhearted and perceptive, holding space without judgment

— A fox, still and watchful, attuned to sound, sensing more than what is said

This day brings healing for those who feel unseen, unheard, or misunderstood ~ and invites us all to give the gift we so deeply crave: sacred presence.

"To truly listen," the day says, "is to offer someone a home for their voice ~ without trying to renovate it."

And quietly, a loop of meaning circles back:

Remember February 6 ~ the Day of Emotional Honesty?

That truth spoken deserves to be heard. Today, you become the space that welcomes it ~ in yourself, in others, in silence.

Later, the soul placed their phone face down. They met someone's eyes for longer than usual.

They listened ~ not to fix, but to *understand*.

Being honest with yourself, ask:

— When do I listen most deeply ~ and how can I bring
   that presence into more of my day?

— What's the difference between listening… and waiting to
   talk?

— What part of me is asking to be heard right now ~ and
   how can I receive it without judgment?

They found connection ~ not by speaking louder, but by *holding
space more softly.*

Sacred Actions: Choose one conversation today ~ even with
yourself ~ where you listen fully. No interruption. No advice.
Just presence. Whisper:

"I am here. I hear you."

Symbolic Focus: The ears, the base of the neck, the space
between inhale and exhale when someone speaks.

Your Mantra for Today ~

"I listen with love. I receive what is true."

March 23 - The Day of Soul Boundaries

A story of choosing what enters, what stays, and what must leave ~ not out of fear, but out of deep self-respect

There once was a soul who said yes when they meant no.

They gave energy they didn't have. They held space they didn't feel safe in. They opened their heart in places where it wasn't honored.

They didn't want to hurt anyone. But in protecting others… they *abandoned themselves.*

One day ~ under the lengthening light of Northern spring, or the rust-gold skies of Southern autumn ~ they stood still and asked:

"What would it look like to love myself enough to draw a line?"

And for the first time, they didn't explain. They didn't apologize. They simply chose.

"This is who I am. This is what I need. This is where I stop."

March 23 carries the energy of 5 (2 + 3), the number of transformation, self-definition, and healthy freedom. In the watery depth of Pisces, this becomes the invitation to hold soul-aligned boundaries ~ the ones that protect your light, not diminish your love.

Boundaries are not walls. They're *filters* ~ that keep your truth intact, your nervous system safe, and your energy *sovereign*.

The archetype of the day is The Boundary Bearer ~ the one who honors their worth enough to say no when needed, and yes only when it's real.

Today's symbols pulse with clarity and care:

— A circle of salt, drawn with reverence, not fear

— Black obsidian, for grounded protection and truth-telling

— The Two of Pentacles, choosing what to carry ~ and what to put down

— A turtle, carrying its home, its edge, and its limits everywhere it goes

This day brings healing for those who've compromised themselves to keep peace. For those who've feared that boundaries would make them "too much" or "not enough."

"Every boundary you set," the day says, "is a blessing to your future self."

And in that inner fortification, a reflection rises:

Remember March 15 ~ the Day of Clear Boundaries?

That was the outer line. Today's is deeper ~ the inner edge where your soul decides what it's truly available for.

Later, the soul took one quiet action. Maybe they said no to a conversation, declined an offer, or honored a body signal. And it didn't feel harsh. It felt *holy*.

Being honest with yourself, ask:

— Where in my life have I allowed something in that no longer aligns?

— What does it feel like when my soul says "no" ~ and how can I respect that?

— How can I hold boundaries not as punishment, but as devotion to my wholeness?

They didn't draw hard lines. They drew *sacred ones.*

Sacred Actions: Name one energetic boundary you're ready to affirm today ~ internally or aloud. Hold it not with defense, but with dignity. Whisper:

"I protect my peace. I choose with love."

Symbolic Focus: The sacral center, the palms pressed outward, the shoulders when standing firm.

Your Mantra for Today ~

"My soul is worthy of protection. My boundaries are love in form."

March 24 ~ The Day of Spiritual Grounding

A story of soul embodiment, rooted presence, and the sacred clarity that comes when spirit meets earth ~ within you

There once was a soul who floated through life.

They were deeply spiritual ~ drawn to intuition, symbols, dreams. They felt everything, imagined more, and often lived *above the noise*.

But eventually, the disconnection caught up. They felt light, but also... untethered. They had insight, but no structure. Peace, but no *presence*.

One day ~ walking through budding earth in the Northern Hemisphere, or beneath trees slowly releasing in the Southern Hemisphere ~ the soul heard a quieter message:

"Come back. Not to pain. Not to pressure. But to your *body*. To your *feet*. To this moment ~ where your spirit lives."

And so they began the return. Not away from spirit ~ but *into it...* fully *embodied.*

March 24 carries the energy of 6 (2 + 4), a number of harmony, embodiment, and healing integration. Under Pisces' mystical influence, this day becomes a powerful call to ground your spirituality ~ not in ritual only, but in *real life.*

This is a day for anchoring intuition into action. For letting your soul live not just in your ideas ~ but in your body, your breath, your choices.

The archetype of the day is The Embodied Spirit ~ the one who walks barefoot, prays with their hands in the soil, and understands that true alignment is not floating away... but *coming fully in.*

Today's symbols carry earthy grace:

— A spiral drawn in soil, encircled by candlelight

— Red jasper, for grounding, vitality, and sacred embodiment

— The Ace of Pentacles, a spiritual seed taking physical root

— A bear, slow, strong, sacred ~ present in both body and intuition

This day brings healing for those who dissociate, who live more in the mind or spirit than the physical world. For those who've separated the mystical from the mundane ~ and are now being called to unite them.

"Your body is not separate from your spirit," the day whispers. "It is the *temple where it lives.*"

And from deep within, a gentle echo rises:

Remember March 7 ~ the Day of Spiritual Integration?

That was the awareness. Today is the anchoring ~ a commitment to let your soul fully inhabit your life.

Later, the soul ate slowly. Touched their own skin with reverence. Walked without rushing. And in that pace, they felt *more spiritual* than ever before.

Being honest with yourself, ask:

— Where have I been floating above my life ~ and how can I return gently to my body?

— What spiritual insights are ready to be lived, not just known?

— What does it feel like to walk through today as if it is a temple?

They didn't abandon spirit. They *rooted it.*

Sacred Actions: Do something physical with sacred attention ~ stretch, cook, touch the earth. Say aloud:

"My body is holy. My life is where my spirit speaks."

Symbolic Focus: The feet pressing into the ground, the lower back, the breath moving downward.

Your Mantra for Today ~

"I ground my spirit. I live my truth in my body."

March 25 - The Day of Soul Restoration

A story of sacred replenishment, emotional recovery, and the quiet power of choosing to heal ~ not because you're broken, but because you're worthy of feeling whole

There once was a soul who kept going.

They showed up when tired. Gave when empty. Smiled when their heart ached.

They believed healing was a luxury. That rest had to be earned. That to stop was to fall behind.

But one day ~ under rain-kissed skies in the North, or soft dusk in the South ~ the soul couldn't keep going. So they *stopped*.

Not in failure. In wisdom.

And in that pause, they felt something return ~ Not energy, not clarity ~ but *themselves*.

"This is what healing feels like," they whispered. "Not fixing... but *restoring.*"

March 25 carries the energy of 7 (2 + 5), the number of inner reflection, emotional depth, and spiritual realignment. In Pisces' soft embrace, this day becomes a pool of restoration ~ an invitation to recover what the pace of life has worn thin.

This is not a day for pushing through. It's a day for pouring back into yourself ~ gently, kindly, without condition.

The archetype of the day is The Soul Restorer ~ the one who knows that healing is cyclical, that silence is sacred, and that tending to the self is not self-indulgence... it is *returning to source.*

Today's symbols soothe and nourish:

— A cup being refilled under a spring, not rushed, not overflowing ~ *enough*

— Amazonite, for emotional balance, soothing boundaries, and calm resilience

— The Four of Swords, a sacred pause for realignment and peace

— A whale, swimming in deep waters ~ slow, wise, undisturbed

This day brings healing for those who carry the weight of "holding it together." For those who've forgotten what it feels like to rest without guilt. For those who are long overdue for *gentle restoration.*

"You do not need to collapse to deserve care," the day says. "You only need to *receive it.*"

And softly, a memory surfaces from within:

Remember February 24 ~ the Day of Embodied Presence? That was your return to the moment. Today is your return to nourishment ~ emotional, energetic, cellular.

Later, the soul wrapped themselves in a blanket. Or turned off their notifications. Or cried without shame.

Being honest with yourself, ask:

— What am I carrying that is no longer mine to hold ~ and what would it feel like to put it down?

— Where am I depleted ~ and how can I begin to restore that gently today?

— What if I let restoration become part of my rhythm, not just a rescue?

They didn't seek answers. They gave themselves *space*.

Sacred Actions: Do one nourishing act today ~ something that restores your energy, not drains it. Whisper:

"I am allowed to heal. I am allowed to rest."

Symbolic Focus: The heart space, the lower belly, the breath in stillness.

Your Mantra for Today ~ *"I restore myself gently. I return to wholeness."*

March 26 - The Day of Living Integrity

A story of inner alignment, soul honesty, and the freedom that comes when your actions, values, and voice all walk in the same direction

There once was a soul who wore many masks.

They weren't fake ~ just fragmented. They spoke one way at work, another at home, and a different way to themselves. They said yes when they meant maybe. They smiled through discomfort.

They thought peace came from keeping things smooth. But deep down, their spirit longed for *truth* ~ not just in words, but in *living*.

One morning ~ beneath spring's clarity in the North, or autumn's quiet refinement in the South ~ they took a breath and asked:

"What would my life look like… if it matched who I *really* am?"

That was the day their soul stopped whispering ~ and began *leading*.

March 26 carries the energy of 8 (2 + 6), the number of personal power, clarity, and ethical alignment. In Pisces' mystical waters, it's easy to drift ~ but this day is a call to come home to your core truth.

Today invites you to close the gap between what you know and what you *do*. Between who you are inside and how you show up in the world.

The archetype of the day is The Soul Aligned One ~ the part of you that speaks the truth not just to others, but to yourself. The one who knows integrity isn't perfection ~ it's *congruence*.

Today's symbols are firm and luminous:

— A single stone placed in the center of a spiral, immovable and true

— Tiger's eye, for courage, protection, and clear action from aligned values

— The King of Swords, a master of clarity, ethics, and thoughtful authority

— A stag, walking straight through a forest path ~ sure, grounded, aware

This day brings healing for those who've been living in fragments, caught between roles, or who fear rejection for being real. For those who have *known the truth for a while* ~ but haven't yet *lived it*.

"You do not have to be perfect," the day says. "You only have to be honest ~ and *live accordingly*."

And a thread loops softly from earlier:

Remember January 26 ~ the Day of Truthful Foundations? That was the knowing. Today is the embodiment ~ a day to walk your truth, not just hold it.

Later, the soul made one decision ~ maybe small, maybe bold ~ that reflected their *real* values. They felt no drama. Just *rightness*.

Being honest with yourself, ask:

— Where am I living out of alignment with my deeper truth?

— What am I pretending not to know ~ and what happens when I finally act on it?

— How can I let integrity be the path, not the pressure?

They didn't get louder. They got *clearer*.

Sacred Actions: Choose one area of your life ~ relationship, habit, or promise ~ and ask:

"Does this match who I really am?"

Take one aligned step toward integrity. Whisper:

"I choose to live my truth."

Symbolic Focus: The throat, the spine, the space between thought and choice.

Your Mantra for Today ~

"My life reflects my truth. My integrity is freedom."

March 27 - The Day of Compassionate Clarity

A story of truth spoken with tenderness, honesty rooted in care, and the strength it takes to be both clear and kind

There once was a soul who struggled to speak up.

They saw the truth, felt the tension, sensed the misalignment ~ but stayed quiet. Not because they didn't care ~ but because they *did*.

They feared hurting someone. Feared being misunderstood. Feared that clarity would cost them connection.

But one moment ~ in a conversation, a mirror, or a journal ~ something shifted. Whether under the brightening skies of Northern spring, or amid the softening light of Southern autumn, the soul said what they had long been holding:

"Here is what's true for me. And I can say it… with love."

It didn't rupture the connection. It *refined* it.

March 27 holds the energy of 9 (2 + 7), the number of wisdom, maturity, and higher truth. Pisces offers emotional depth ~ and today asks that your truth be shaped not by impulse or defensiveness, but by *compassion*.

This is not a day for brutal honesty. It's a day for brave kindness ~ the kind that respects both your voice and someone else's heart.

The archetype of the day is The Gentle Truth-Teller ~ the one who knows that clarity doesn't require coldness. That the highest form of communication includes *presence, boundaries, and care*.

Today's symbols speak with warmth and precision:

— A quill dipped in soft ink, writing clearly on handmade paper

— Blue lace agate, for gentle truth and harmonious communication

— The Justice card, balanced truth rooted in fairness and heart

— A dove, flying low ~ peaceful, clear-eyed, carrying a message of truth

This day brings healing for those who bite their tongue out of love, or who've been taught that clarity equals cruelty. For those who've been on either side of silence ~ and are ready to speak *with compassion*.

"You can be honest without being harsh," the day says. "You can be clear and still be kind."

And softly, a memory flows forward:

Remember March 6 ~ the Day of Restorative Honesty? That was the beginning of truth spoken gently. Today, it becomes a skill. A choice. A gift you offer yourself and others. *

Later, the soul paused before a difficult truth ~ and chose to speak it anyway, not to win, not to prove ~ but to *heal*.

Being honest with yourself, ask:

— Where have I been avoiding honesty because I'm afraid of the impact ~ not because it's untrue?

— How can I say what I need to say with love ~ not armor?

— What part of me needs clarity ~ not to divide, but to bring things back into harmony?

They didn't shout. They *shared*.

Sacred Actions: Speak one gentle truth today ~ to yourself or someone else. Let it come from love, not fear. Whisper:

"I can be kind and clear at the same time."

Symbolic Focus: The throat, the lips just before speaking, the heart after being honest.

Your Mantra for Today ~

"My truth is clear. My truth is kind. My truth heals."

March 28 - The Day of Sacred Discipline

A story of quiet structure, devoted repetition, and the soul-deep knowing that consistency is a form of self-respect

There once was a soul who resisted routine.

They longed to be free ~ unbound, spontaneous, ever inspired. They feared discipline would cage them. That structure would smother creativity. That commitment would steal joy.

But over time, the soul noticed something else. The ideas came… but drifted. The dreams bloomed… but never rooted.

One day ~ beneath emerging blossoms in the North, or falling leaves in the South ~ they chose something different.

They repeated a practice. They created a rhythm. They showed up ~ even when it wasn't convenient.

"This," the soul whispered, "isn't rigidity. It's reverence."

March 28 holds the vibration of 1 (2 + 8 = 10 → 1), the number of beginnings, clarity, and sovereign action. But in Pisces' dreamy sea, that energy requires *anchoring* ~ or it floats away.

Today invites you to create sacred containers for your becoming. Not to constrain your soul ~ but to give it *something to grow in.*

The archetype of the day is The Devoted One ~ the part of you who shows up for your dreams not just when it's easy, but when it's meaningful.

The one who knows that self-love isn't always soft ~ sometimes, it looks like *discipline.*

Today's symbols are steady, sacred, and simple:

— A candle lit at the same hour each day, its flame growing deeper, not taller

— Garnet, for commitment, rooted energy, and devotion to inner truth

— The Hierophant card, wisdom through ritual, lineage, and sacred repetition

— A monk walking a labyrinth, one mindful step at a time

— A worn journal opened to the same page each morning, edges softened by devotion

— A stone basin collecting rain — not rushed, just filled through quiet constancy

This day brings healing for those who avoid structure out of past restriction ~ or who've mistaken freedom for lack of rhythm. For those whose inner brilliance now craves an outer form.

"Your soul doesn't need more pressure," the day says. "It needs a place to land."

And softly, a memory resurfaces:

Remember January 28 ~ the Day of Sustainable Will? That inner fire you lit? Today is how you sustain it ~ not in bursts, but in rhythm.

Later, the soul did one thing they didn't feel like doing ~ not out of guilt, but *devotion.*

They followed through. And felt grounded, not constrained.

Being honest with yourself, ask:

— What part of me would thrive with more sacred consistency?

— Where do I resist discipline ~ and what belief is hiding underneath that?

— How can I create a rhythm that holds me without hardening me?

They didn't become rigid. They became *rooted.*

Sacred Actions: Choose one nourishing habit today ~ and commit to it gently for the next 7 days. Not as a rule, but as a ritual. Whisper:

"I show up for what matters. I am a vessel for what I value."

Symbolic Focus: The base of the spine, the hands in practice, the breath when steady and paced.

Your Mantra for Today ~

"My devotion is discipline. My structure is sacred."

March 29 - The Day of Inner Release

A story of gentle surrender, emotional unclenching, and the quiet liberation that happens when you stop holding what no longer holds you

There once was a soul who carried too much.

Old guilt. Unspoken grief. Expectations that were never theirs to begin with.

They kept it close ~ in their shoulders, their breath, their sleep. They didn't even know how much weight they held until something small broke open.

Maybe a soft word. A song. A breeze during early spring in the North or the hush of twilight in the South.

Whatever it was, it opened a door inside them.

"I don't need to keep this," the soul whispered. "I can let go ~ not in anger, but in *love*."

And so, they released. Not everything. Just enough. Enough to feel *free*.

March 29 carries the energy of 2 (2 + 9 = 11 → 1 + 1 = 2), the number of emotional presence, surrender, and relational healing. In Pisces ~ the sign of endings, flow, and mystic transition ~ this becomes a deeply cleansing day.

Not the kind of purge that's dramatic or loud. But a quiet opening. A releasing of what's tight. A sacred *unclenching*.

The archetype of the day is The Inner Liberator ~ the one who chooses peace over control, who releases stories that are no longer true, and who trusts that letting go *isn't loss* ~ it's alignment.

Today's symbols soften and dissolve:

— A single leaf drifting downriver, unresisted

— Smoky quartz, for energetic release and clearing old patterns

— The Death card, transformation through surrender, not destruction

— A snake shedding skin, not in pain ~ but in readiness

— A melting icicle, drop by drop, returning to the flow without force

— An exhale in winter air, visible for a moment ~then released to stillness

This day brings healing for those who hold on because it feels safer than surrender. For those who've confused endurance with wholeness. For those who are ready to exhale ~ maybe for the first time in a while.

"You are not what you release," the day says.

"You are what remains ~ *truer, clearer, lighter.*"

And as that breath deepens, a reflection stirs:

Remember February 28 ~ the Day of Sacred Closure? That was a farewell. Today is a follow-through ~ a release not of grief, but of gratitude.

Later, the soul lit a candle and named what they no longer needed. They cried. They smiled. They felt the space that opened when they no longer had to carry everything.

Being honest with yourself, ask:

— What have I been holding onto out of habit, fear, or guilt?

— What would happen if I gave myself permission to let it go ~ gently, today?

— What part of me is asking to be free ~ even if I still love what I'm releasing?

They didn't run. They *released* ~ with grace.

Sacred Actions: Write one sentence that begins, *"I no longer need…"* and complete it honestly. Burn or bury it if you feel called. Whisper:

"I let go with love. I make space for what's true."

Symbolic Focus: The shoulders, the chest during an exhale, the hands when turned open to the sky.

Your Mantra for Today ~

"I release with grace. I trust what flows away."

March 30 - The Day of Emergence and Purpose

A story of quiet direction, soul-centered clarity, and the moment when purpose stops being a destination ~ and becomes something you live

There once was a soul who searched for purpose like a buried treasure.

They read books. Took quizzes. Asked others: "What am I here to do?"

Sometimes, they caught glimpses ~ flashes of alignment, moments of meaning ~ but they still waited for the big answer.

Until one day ~ under warming winds in the North, or cooling skies in the South ~ they stopped asking "what," and started asking *"where am I already living with meaning?"*

They listened. And realized…

"Purpose isn't something I find. It's something I *notice*. And then *choose* ~ every day."

March 30 carries the energy of 3 (3 + 0), the number of direction, self-expression, and aligned motion. With Pisces nearing its final notes, this day hums with soul-centered clarity ~ not as an endpoint, but a *living path*.

You're not here to chase your purpose like it's hiding. You're here to live in a way that lets it *reveal itself* through you.

The archetype of the day is The Purpose-Bearer ~ not the one who declares a title or mission, but the one who lives with quiet intention. Whose every yes and no becomes a thread in a meaningful tapestry.

Today's symbols inspire gentle certainty:

— A compass resting on a heart, pulsing gently

— Sunstone, for vital alignment, confidence, and embodied intention

— The Three of Wands, looking forward with calm trust in what's unfolding

— A hawk in flight, not circling ~ but gliding with clarity of aim

This day brings healing for those who've felt lost in comparison, pressured to define their calling, or burdened by the myth that purpose must be loud and impressive.

"You don't need a mission statement," the day says. "You only need a truth that feels like home ~ and the courage to *follow it*."

And softly, a soul thread lifts from earlier:

Remember March 21 ~ the Day of Soul Momentum? That first movement has matured. Today, your direction clarifies ~ not by force, but by emergence.

Later, the soul looked at what they were already doing. The way they listen. The way they create. The way they show up ~ consistently, imperfectly, *meaningfully*.

Being honest with yourself, ask:

— Where in my life do I already feel purposeful ~ even if I've never called it that?

— What lights me up from within ~ and how can I follow that more deliberately?

— What if my purpose wasn't a thing I chased, but a truth I embodied ~ one small choice at a time?

They didn't find their path. They *realized they were already walking it.*

Sacred Actions: Write down three things you've done recently that felt meaningful. Then whisper:

"This is purpose. This is enough."

Choose one small act today that continues that thread ~ consciously.

Symbolic Focus: The chest, the lower spine, the fingertips during a purposeful gesture.

Your Mantra for Today ~

"I live my purpose in the choices I make. It begins in me."

March 31 - The Day of Inner Completion

A story of full-circle stillness, soul acknowledgment, and the peace that arises when you realize ~ you don't need to begin again, you just need to recognize how far you've come*

There once was a soul who kept searching for closure.

They thought it would look like an answer. A clear ending. A ribbon tied around the past. They believed completion had to be earned ~ through effort, achievement, or proof.

But one quiet evening ~ as spring awakened in the North and autumn deepened in the South ~ the soul stood still.

There was no big finish. No revelation. Just a sense of arrival… in their own skin.

"I'm not waiting anymore," they thought. "I've already arrived ~ not at perfection, but *at presence*."

And in that moment, what felt unfinished… finally made sense.

March 31 carries the energy of 4 (3 + 1), the number of grounded completion, inner order, and reflection. As the final day of Pisces ~ and the close of Volume 1, *Seeds of Stillness* ~ this day honors all you've planted, remembered, released, and reclaimed.

It asks nothing of you. It offers *space* ~ to acknowledge, integrate, and breathe.

The archetype of the day is The Whole Self ~ the part of you that no longer rushes into the next chapter, but sits quietly with what this one has taught you. The part of you that sees the beauty in *being whole, not finished.*

Today's symbols are restful and real:

— A circle drawn in soil, one handprint in the center ~ marked, soft, whole

— The World card, signifying completion, fulfillment, and a new kind of beginning

— A butterfly on a stone, wings still, no longer transforming ~ simply *being*

This day brings healing for those who always chase the next breakthrough, who have struggled to rest in what is, or who fear that pausing means losing momentum.

"Completion," the day says, "is not an ending. It's a return ~ to truth, to self, to peace."

And with deep resonance, a final loop connects:

Remember January 1 ~ the Day of Sacred Thresholds? You stepped in with intention. Today, you step back ~ *with understanding.*

Not a circle closing. A spiral completing its first turn.

Later, the soul looked back ~ not in regret, but reverence. They honored their own becoming. Not all fixed. Not all done. But *honestly integrated.*

Being honest with yourself, ask:

— What has shifted in me since I began this journey ~ not on the outside, but within?

— What can I name, release, or carry forward with gratitude today?

— How can I mark this quiet ending ~ not as a goodbye, but as a sacred completion?

They didn't need to begin again. They needed only to *witness their wholeness.*

Sacred Actions: Light a candle or sit quietly. Name aloud three ways you have changed ~ inwardly. No rush. No need to fix. Whisper:

"I am whole. I honor this chapter. I am ready ~ for what unfolds next."

Symbolic Focus: The crown, the soles of the feet, the breath between what ends and begins.

Your Mantra for Today ~

"I have become more of myself. I complete this with peace."

March Reflection

Through the Veil is a Soul's Inventory at the Edge of the Unknown

You've moved through a month of unveiling. Not a linear path ~ but a spiral. Not always graceful ~ but honest.

March asked more of you. Not in volume ~ but in *depth*. It stirred what was hidden. Called forward old stories. Held a mirror to the face behind the mask ~ and gently said:

"You're ready to see what you've outgrown."

This is not a month to "summarize." It is a moment to *witness* what surfaced.

Soul Inventory: What Has Been Revealed?

Allow this to be spacious. Raw. Unfiltered.

— What truth emerged that surprised or unsettled me?

— What did I let go of this month ~ willingly or not ~ that was no longer aligned?

— Which inner voice became louder ~ and which one did I finally question?

— Where did I feel the presence of my shadow ~ and what did I learn from it?

— What veil was lifted ~ and what did I see more clearly than before?

Honoring the Unknown

Sometimes the gift of March is *not* clarity ~ but clarity about what is *not yours to carry forward*.

Reflect:

— Where am I still in the dark ~ and can I allow that to be sacred, not shameful?

— What uncertainty am I learning to walk with, not fix?

— What part of me feels more whole now that I've stopped pretending to know everything?

Integration Invitation

Create a "Veil Page."

At the back of your journal or in a blank space, title one page:

What I Saw When I Looked Deeper.

No pressure. Just write what comes ~ images, memories, symbols, feelings. This page is private. Sacred. A mirror you *earned* the right to look into.

Then ask:

What part of me did I meet this month ~ and what part of me did I reclaim?

Let mystery be your ally, not your fear.

Closing Mantra for March

"I no longer fear the unknown.

I walk with it.

What I have unveiled cannot be unseen.

I am not lost ~ I am becoming visible to myself."

Notes

Your Journey Continues...

Congratulations!

You've arrived at the end of *Seeds of Stillness* ~ not as a finish line, but as a foundation. For 90 days, you've slowed down, listened in, and rooted your soul in the sacred rhythm of presence.

— You've met yourself in silence.

— You've paused before performance.

— You've remembered that growth doesn't begin with a roar ~ it begins with a breath.

But something has started to stir beneath the surface, hasn't it?

There is a rhythm gathering strength now ~ a quiet opening in your chest, a warming under the skin, a whisper asking,

"What if I softened even more… and bloomed?"

That's where *Volume 2 ~ Origins of Opening* begins.

The next 90 days are not about rushing forward ~ they are about unfolding inward.

They are about emotional intimacy, sensual awakening, creative courage, and vulnerable trust.

— If Volume 1 taught you how to arrive...

— Volume 2 will show you how to open.

You are not who you were three months ago. You are not behind. You are exactly where your soul is ready to expand.

So take one more breath.

Open the book.

And begin again ~ not as a stranger, but as someone *returning home to their own becoming.*